Writing against Racial Injury

Pittsburgh Series in Composition, Literacy, and Culture

David Bartholomae and Jean Ferguson Carr, Editors

Writing against Racial Injury

The Politics of Asian American Student Rhetoric

Haivan V. Hoang

University of Pittsburgh Press

Published by the University of Pittsburgh Press, Pittsburgh, Pa., 15260
Copyright © 2015, University of Pittsburgh Press
All rights reserved
Manufactured in the United States of America
Printed on acid-free paper
10 9 8 7 6 5 4 3 2 1

ISBN 10: 0-8229-6362-0
ISBN 13: 978-0-8229-6362-2

Cataloging-in-Publication data is available from the Library of Congress.

Contents

Acknowledgments

This research project has taken me on a winding and unanticipated path: first exploring ethnographies of communication among Asian American activists in California; then turning back toward a related historiography of Asian American student publications and Asian American studies scholarship; then to judicial cases, critical race theory, and American studies; and finally, returning to my readers in the present—a readership that will, I hope, cut across the fields of literacy studies, ethnic minority rhetorics, translingual perspectives, Asian American studies, and racial theories. Throughout this journey, I have had the good fortune to learn from, work with, and be supported by generous colleagues, family members, and friends.

The Asian/Asian American Caucus, part of the broader National Council of Teachers of English, has been a home for me as a scholar. With the support of this community, I have been encouraged to ask critical questions about Asian American speakers and writers and their/our experiences with language, literacy, and rhetoric and to find ways to critically listen to these experiences. I have found camaraderie with colleagues asking related questions in different moments and places. As a whole, this caucus has nurtured and continues to nurture important work on Asian American writing as well as a sense of solidarity among those pursuing such work.

I would be remiss if I did not convey special thanks to those leaders, mentors, and colleagues who've sustained me from the beginning of this project: LuMing Mao, who invited me to my first caucus meeting and always offered kind words of support; Morris Young, who shared his page proofs of *Minor Re/Visions* so that I would have at least one work on Asian American literacy cited in my dissertation and continued to give generous support; and Terese Guinsatao Monberg, whose research on oral histories of Filipino/a American rhetors inspired me to listen more critically and who, over the years, has become a friend as well as a colleague. For more than a decade, all three have been more than encouraging of this project and my professional career.

I am grateful to those who've supported me more locally, first at Ohio State University and then at the University of Massachusetts Amherst. This project began as a dissertation, an ethnographic case study of the discourse practices of a Vietnamese American student organization, written during my graduate studies at Ohio State. I deeply appreciate the thoughtful comments and generative dialogue that I had with my dissertation committee: Beverly J. Moss, Andrea Lunsford, Brenda Brueggemann, and Amy Shuman. As my adviser, Beverly challenged me to pursue ethnographies of literacy in racial minority communities and to think critically about how these are situated more broadly in the field; reading her honest, critical responses to my research, I knew that I could trust her praise as well as her critiques.

In 2004, I was fortunate to join a strong community of scholars in composition and rhetoric at UMass Amherst, a community that grew to include additional colleagues who made our group more vibrant. The university generously supported me through the Faculty Research Grant, which funded travel to university archives as well as a pre-tenure leave in order to work on this manuscript. The faculty community there gave me intellectual support. In particular, I thank Donna LeCourt and Anne Herrington, who welcomed me in 2004, saw enough potential in my work to give me a job (!), and read and commented on portions of this book. I have a deep respect for their scholarship and the generosity and care with which they approach research inquiry, teaching, and mentoring; for this reason, their encouragement has been incredibly meaningful, fortifying me to work through and, at long last, complete this manuscript.

I am also grateful for the student activists in the Vietnamese American Coalition (VAC), who welcomed me into their community and shared their thoughts and rhetorical practices with me. VAC was far from homogeneous, but what these students shared was a curiosity about their place as Asian Americans in the world and a desire to express their multivalent selves.

Finally, I am indebted to my family. Growing up with my parents, brothers, and sisters in California in the post–civil rights and post–Vietnam War era has given me good perspective on what it means to be Vietnamese American and has inspired me to pursue questions about what it means to be Asian American in the United States. And I cannot even express how grateful I am for my husband, Cedric, who has unconditionally supported and sustained me throughout this project, and my daughter, Josie, whose love has helped me keep this world in perspective.

Writing against Racial Injury

Introduction

Literacy, Race, and an American Ethos

If we reflect on the history of language and literacy education in the United States, we will surely find deep contradiction. Reading and writing—particularly in "proper," middle-class English—was widely believed to foster virtue, progress, and democratic ideals, but for those who have been racially othered, the right to literacy was often spirited out of reach. The double bind for racial minorities was particularly egregious in the antebellum period, when literacy, upheld as a testament to one's humanity, was sponsored by Christian missionaries at the same time that it was violently withheld from African Americans by slave owners. Indeed, contradiction punctuates the history of U.S. literacy as racism continued to undo the promise of literacy education. Research in the past few decades has documented patterns of racial injustice in the United States at least since the nineteenth century: school segregation based on race and language background; nativist suppression of ethnic language schools; discriminatory use of literacy and language tests to exclude minorities from voting rights, jury service, and naturalized citizenship; and educational policies and pedagogies that penalize linguistic and rhetorical differences that do not emulate standard American English and U.S. academic writing conventions. In short, racial injury persisted in language and literacy education in at least two essential ways: one, such education was withheld and two, when acquired, sanctioned standards for linguistic performance held ethnic minority difference in low esteem.

But it is not only the *past* of racial injury that should concern educators these days. What reading and writing teachers and researchers need to understand is that racial ideologies clutch onto the *present* and abide in our cultural beliefs about language and literacy, and we have yet to fully examine how such beliefs inform the ethos that speakers and writers are asked to inhabit. Understanding the ways in which race continues to burden language and literacy education is particularly important when we recognize that struggles for racial accountability are now hampered by the belief that we live in a postracial society where race no longer matters, by the ways in which language and literacy difference have become tropes for racial discrimination, and by the fact that linguistic diversity in our schools is rising at the same time that we face mounting pressure to standardize students' language and writing practices. The imperative for us now is to examine how the past follows, clings to, and intrudes upon the *present.* In this post-1960s era, in this half-century aftermath of dramatic civil rights struggles and legislative reform, how do racial injuries return to burden language and literacy education and practices? And in what ways can we work toward a rhetoric that at once remembers legacies of racism *and* works hopefully toward racial accountability?

For a glimpse at the tenacity of these racial legacies, we might pause briefly to examine how post-1960s language ideologies are gracefully depicted in the opening pages of Chang-Rae Lee's novel *Native Speaker.* Early in the novel, Korean American Henry Park reminisces over his first flirtations with Lelia Boswell, a self-described "average white girl" whom he would eventually marry. Slipping away from a crowded party, the two share tequila and intimate talk in a park filled with a pleasant mix of Spanish and English:

> "People like me are always thinking about still having an accent," I said, trying to remember the operation of the salt, the liquor, the lime.
> "I can tell," she said.
> I asked her how.
> "You speak perfectly, of course. I mean if we were talking on the phone, I wouldn't think twice."
> "You mean it's my face."
> "No, it's not that," she answered. She reached over as if to touch my cheek

but rested her arm instead on the bench back, grazing my neck. "You look like someone half listening to himself. You pay attention to what you're doing. If I had to guess, you're not a native speaker. Say something."

"What should I say?"

"Say my name."

"Lelia," I said. "Lelia."

"See? You said *Leel-ya* so deliberately. You tried not to but you were taking in the syllables. You're very careful." (11)

The double-consciousness that "people like me" inhabit is a reminder of the ways that language and literacy have been used in the service of racial injury and registers the wariness that remains. Indeed, Henry's awareness and self-scrutiny as a racialized subject is more unrelenting than Lelia could have imagined in the early days of their relationship. As a child, he sees himself through the derisive eyes of a seemingly perfect white girl and patterns his speech after hers. Later, he is the one to discipline racial others when a firm hires him to spy on "foreign workers, immigrants, first-generationals, and neo-Americans" considered threats to powerful clients, and he is unsettled as he betrays new immigrants through his *writing*. He writes and relinquishes to unknown, powerful clients "the tract of their [new immigrants'] lives, unauthorized biographies" (16).

Henry and Lelia's conversation anticipates the ways the two will struggle in their marriage not only because of *his* caution with language but hers as well. Lelia is a speech therapist who explains why *she* is so careful with language: "Unfortunately, I am the standard-bearer"(11). As a therapist, she recognizes that she occupies the traditional raced and gendered position of teacher and "standard-bearer," one that is meant to nurture and educate English-language learners toward normative ways of speaking and listening. A long history of discriminatory language education entangles their marriage until, eventually, Lelia leaves Henry, placing in his hands a list of "who he is." Finding a stray postscript—"false speaker of language"—prompts him to reflect: "Naturally, I came to see the list as indicative of her failures as well as mine. What we shared. It was the list of our sad children" (13). Here are two people who, encumbered by a messy racial inheritance, struggle to remake the "native speaker" and its "false" partner and, in doing so, stumble toward reconciliation within themselves and with one another.

It is telling that *Native Speaker* begins with separation and then devotes the remaining pages to the search for a healing language. Even as language and literacy education has become more widely accessible over the past century, we still find traces of racial injury in the double-consciousness of language minorities like Henry as well as in the carefulness of white and nonwhite language educators like Lelia. After all, as Deborah Brandt tells us, "rapid changes in literacy and language may not so much bring rupture from the past as they bring an accumulation of different and proliferating pasts, a piling up of literate artifacts and signifying practices that haunt the sites of literacy learning" ("Accumulating" 665). In light of these ghostly returns, it is apparent that racial injury in language and literacy education can no longer be understood solely in terms of exclusion and other blatant acts of racism. In fact, as quite a few race scholars have argued, the emphasis on injury in race discourse—particularly, as Carl Gutiérrez-Jones asserts, on injuries of exclusion—tends to foreground isolated grievances and obscure legacies of systemic racial formation. Gutiérrez-Jones further contends that we must think more critically about the *nature* of racial injury. Racial injury, I argue, takes form not only as discrete discriminatory acts but also as the accumulation of racializing acts that precede, pile up, and perform on "native" and racial minority writers and speakers alike. What language and literacy educators need now is an understanding of the ways these "proliferating pasts" have come to constitute the subject positions available to racial minority writers as well as prevalent beliefs about the literate American ideal.

Writing against Racial Injury: The Politics of Asian American Student Rhetoric begins by exploring the racialization of the American speaking and writing subject. More specifically, this book asks what we can learn about this ethos from the story of Asian American activism for language and literacy rights in post-1960s California. The politics of Asian American education, I believe, can shed light on the historical struggle between the hope that we place in language and literacy education and the racial legacies that have frustrated that hope. By the late 1960s, the Asian American movement had inspired in race-conscious activists fresh optimism toward education and the promise of a collective voice. Asian American activists would pursue racial justice *through* their writing and, moreover, advocate *for* language and literacy as a form of racial accountability.

This activism, however, is hardly perceptible in the public imagination since Asian Americans—racialized as model minorities (read: already assimilated and thus invisible) or as perpetual foreigners (read: outside the nation's history)—are seldom recognized as full participants in American cultural production. But the truth is that America's national history of folding Asian Americans into economic realms as laborers and commercial partners while estranging them from political membership has created what Lisa Lowe has called "an alternative site, a site of cultural forms that propose, enact, and embody subjects and practices not contained by the narrative of American citizenship" (176). For this reason, considering Asian American cultural production in these alternative sites is essential to identifying the forms that racial injury now takes. By exploring Asian American activist rhetoric at the sites of language and literacy production, I seek to understand the ways past racial injury has shaped common notions about who has the authority to speak and write as an American.

This book is concerned with the formation of the literate American ethos and its rearticulation by Asian American activists who, in the post–civil rights era, contested constraints on their language and literacy rights and composed an Asian American rhetoric to reimagine the American subject on more just terms. To understand the impetus for Asian American activism for language and literacy rights, we begin by examining why language and literacy became so deeply entrenched in our sense of American selfhood. Next we look at how Asian Americans were fashioned as outsider to that ethos.

THE GOOD AMERICAN WRITING WELL: LITERACY AND A RACIALIZED ETHOS

> To think of literacy as a staple of life—on the order of indoor lights or clothing— is to understand how thoroughly most Americans in these times are able to take their literacy for granted. It is also to appreciate how central reading and writing can be to people's sense of security and well-being, *even to their sense of dignity*.
>
> —DEBORAH BRANDT, *LITERACY IN AMERICAN LIVES* 1 (EMPHASIS MINE)

The promise of language and literacy education has been fundamental to the invention of an ideal American ethos throughout U.S. history. Reading and writing was and is commonly understood to cultivate a "sense of dignity" and good character—an assumption akin to the emphasis on the "good man speaking well" in the classical rhetorical tradition. To be sure, the meaning of "good" has and will change across cultures and historical moments, but even as social conditions have altered, the belief that literacy education enriches the American self and the wider public remains steadfast. Put another way, a commonplace about literacy has persisted throughout American history: the belief that we read and write to better ourselves and, further, to better society. Literacy, then, is not simply about the coding and decoding of written linguistic systems, but it also must be understood as text-based engagement with a society that attributes to literacy the power to further our most dearly held cultural values. Yet even as literacy has been seen as a categorical public good in the formation of an American ethos, literacy was at the same time a site of racial injury.

The cultural significance of literacy, as Sylvia Scribner has explained in her seminal essay "Literacy in Three Metaphors," can be understood through three basic metaphors: literacy as adaptation, literacy as power, and literacy as grace. Whereas "literacy-as-adaptation" attends to the practical uses of reading and writing, the emphasis on the pragmatic tends to obscure the symbolic meaning that literacy has for people across many cultures: grace and power. "Literacy-as-grace" refers to the belief that literacy fosters virtue within the individual (13–15). In the United States, from the colonial era through the nineteenth-century Sunday school movement, literacy was considered essential to salvation for Christian missionaries and everyday believers. Women were responsible for teaching their children to read the Bible, missionaries sought to teach slaves and Native Americans to read in churches and schoolhouses, and Sunday schools provided literacy education to those who could not attend town schools (Boylan; Gordon and Gordon; Monaghan). Moreover, the assumption that literacy can nurture virtue was certainly not restricted to the religious. As Scribner writes, the "notion that participation in a literate—that is, bookish—tradition enlarges and develops a person's essential self is pervasive and still undergirds the concept of a liberal education" (13).

The belief that literacy would strengthen moral and intellectual virtue became fundamental to the new nation. It seemed that literacy education would foster virtue in the self that might, in turn, enable Americans to enrich society through political, socioeconomic, and cultural means. Within the young nation, debates over the establishment of a national language academy were spurred on by the belief in "literacy-as-power," or the promise that literacy would foster civic engagement and social progress. Political leaders, for the most part, believed that literacy would encourage the spread of democracy, showcase scientific advances, and eventually yield a national literature. John Adams thus proposed establishing a national language academy that would emphasize English-language development, Benjamin Franklin cautioned against German-language schools, and Noah Webster created dictionaries and textbooks to promote an American English. Many early leaders, however, contended that tolerance for diverse languages would be most conducive to the growth of the nation and that adopting a single national language would be too reminiscent of monarchical rule (Heath, "Why No Official Tongue?"). At the same time, as Dennis Baron has argued, these early efforts register an emergent ideology that associated the English language in particular with national identity and progress (*English-Only Question*).

To become lettered *in English,* then, was to become an American self whose virtue was defined by morality, intellectual talent, civic engagement, and socioeconomic worth. The growth of common schools and then public universities in the nineteenth century reaffirmed this ideology of language and literacy. Moreover, English language and literacy became fundamental to citizenship rights as Edward Stevens Jr. so thoroughly delineates through American legal history. The hope that inspired literacy, however, was tempered by a related denial that frustrated language and literacy education for racial minorities. If literacy symbolized the path toward becoming the "good" American, then legacies of racism undoubtedly seated racial minorities in opposition to this ethos. A troubling alternation between promise and denial would sadly come to typify literacy education.

Language and literacy education for Native Americans and African Americans until the nineteenth century, for instance, was often cast in terms of spiritual edification but effectively positioned white missionaries as the bearers of grace and racial minorities as wanting in virtue. From praying towns in the colonies to government-sponsored boarding schools, white missionaries were devoted to Native American literacy education because they hoped for the religious conversion of those they considered unsaved and uncivilized. Many of the most prominent missionaries and educators—such as Puritans John Eliot and the Mayhew family, the Franciscan friars in the Catholic missions, and Lt. Richard Pratt of the Carlisle Indian Industrial School—also encouraged the *cultural* conversion of these students (Enoch; Gordon and Gordon 193–225). Cultivation of the good American often went against indigenous cultural traditions, and this is apparent in Edward Gordon and Elaine Gordon's account of Iroquois experiences at the Boyle Indian School: "Benjamin Franklin was told by the Iroquois that students who had 'been educated in that college . . . were absolutely good for nothing . . . for killing deer, catching beaver or surprising an enemy.' For they had forgotten the 'true methods' of the Indians. Instead, Franklin tells us that the Iroquois proposed that English children be sent to them. The Iroquois, 'would take care of their Education, bring them up . . . and make men of them'" (200). Education was about ushering Native Americans into a white mainstream notion of Christian faith and cultural identification.

Likewise, white missionaries advocated for the literacy education of slaves, and despite the protests of slave owners who feared revolt, the belief that reading is vital to one's spiritual life was persistent enough that churches became major sponsors of African American literacy. In her history of African American literacy education in the antebellum era, Janet Duitsman Cornelius writes that many slaves from West African cultures likely already had a high regard for literacy, and their enslavement meant that writing petitions to the courts and narratives to the public would become important in their fight for freedom. As churches continued to encourage literacy, African Americans who belonged to Baptist and Methodist congregations in particular made the most of opportunities to become leaders and promote the cultural life of fellow congregants. But by the late nineteenth century, several states made it illegal to teach slaves to read, and many evangelicals who supported the literacy education of slaves assented to the institution of slavery. In sum, language and literacy education for Native Americans and African Americans at once sought to foster moral virtue and assumed that they lacked such virtue. More broadly, literacy education meant to foster a kind of moral virtue that ushered students into racial, gendered, and class-based norms.

Later, in the twentieth century, even as opportunities for literacy education started to develop, literacy continued to be a site of racial injury. In the racial anxieties that followed the Civil War, literacy tests were unevenly administered and effectively disenfranchised many African Americans from the right to vote (Stevens; Kates). Schools for African Americans and other racial minorities suffered from poor facilities, few resources, and little funding. And by the late 1960s, dialect, language, and other cultural differences were unjustly assessed as intellectual deficiency and a social failure on the part of parents and communities, leading to the inordinate placement of African American children in special education classes (Ball and Lardner; Labov). Finally, there are the racial anxieties that percolate in contemporary conflicts over Black English and other nonstandard dialects, bilingual education, and national language policy.

Literacy education in the United States has clearly played a powerful part in the racial legacies that educators have inherited. Racial injury took the form of outright denial of education, segregated schools, poor material conditions in "colored" schools, and discriminatory standards for linguistic performance. What's more is that each act of racial injury piled up such that racial minorities were interpellated into subject positions estranged from the good American writing well. After all, literacy has symbolized American virtues—moral, political, socioeconomic, cultural, and cognitive—that, as Catherine Prendergast has argued, became coupled with whiteness (*Literacy and Racial Justice*). By contrast, mainstream literacy education had long started with the assumption that racial minorities and working-class whites fell short of all those virtues that reading and writing symbolized. Writing as the ideal American self was difficult as nonwhite people were racialized based on moral, political, socioeconomic, cultural, and cognitive terms. As constraining as racial formation has been, it is remarkable that there have been so many notable minority speakers and writers who contested these subject positions and still turned to the power of reading, writing, and speaking to find voice, create art, and demand social justice. The past few decades have seen histories and ethnographies of literacy that document lived literacy practices and the cultural significance that reading and writing have for diverse ethnic communities.

But often missing from these critical histories of literacy education and practice are Asian Americans. The silence about Asian Americans might be explained by the unfailing construction of Asian immigrants and their American-born children as always foreign, always foil to an ideal American ethos. The question is often not whether Asian Americans can write as *good* Americans so much as whether they can write as *Americans at all.* As a result, Asian Americans—and Latino/a Americans, for that matter—tend to be missing from mainstream narratives about American culture. Even as Asian American language and literacy education and practices are often cast in shadow, it is nonetheless important to read their stories in the context of the wider history of literacy and in relation to the racial formation of other minorities. The patterns in racial injury against Asian Americans were similarly disconcerting in that Asian Americans have been constructed as being outsider to the literate American ethos based on moral, political, cultural, and cognitive grounds. While little has been written about Asian Americans in literacy studies, we can look to Asian American studies and histories of education to learn about the racial injury that Asian Americans had to endure in public schools and the impact that this must have had on Asian American language and literacy education.

RACIAL INJURY IN ASIAN AMERICAN EDUCATION

> The duty which the teachers owe to the children committed to their charge should prompt them to active efforts to save the rising generation from contamination and pollution by *a race reeking with the vices of the Orient, a race that knows neither truth, principle, modesty nor respect for our laws.* The moral and physical ruin already wrought to our youth by contact with these people is fearful.
>
> Let us exhaust all peaceful methods to stop its spread.
>
> —San Francisco school superintendent Andrew Moulder in 1886,
> qtd. in Victor Low, The Unimpressible Race (74, emphasis mine)

The politics of Asian American education, in many ways, mirrored the legacies of racism imposed on other racial minorities, and such discrimination is aptly captured by the 1886 statement of San Francisco school superintendent (and former California State school superintendent) Andrew Moulder's 1886 statement against admitting Chinese children into the public schools. The denigration of the virtue of Chinese, Japanese, and other Asian immigrants and their American-born children reflected a deep nativism against the "Mongolian" race and related anxieties over American language and literacy education. What's clear is that public education is partly responsible for the racial formation of Asian Americans, and more than a century of racial injury in the schools provided the impetus for the rising activism for language and literacy education that grew fervent in the late 1960s.

The concerted struggles over Asian American education are best understood within the context of the Asian migrations that began gathering momentum three decades prior to Moulder's remarks. The mid-nineteenth through the early twentieth century saw approximately one million Chinese, Japanese, Filipino, Korean, and Indian immigrants arrive in Hawaii, California, and the Pacific Northwest. Interestingly, as Sucheng Chan points out in *Asian Americans: An Interpretive History,* this transnational migration was partly set in motion by the West's imperialist interventions in the East: the Opium War led to British power within China's ports and, as a result, damaged cottage industries and opportunities for local workers; the United States similarly induced Japan into opening up to trade in the Treaty of 1854; the Spanish-American War resulted in American acquisition of the Philippines despite Filipino struggles for independence; and British colonialism in India produced new diasporic migrations through Hong Kong and to other parts of Asia, the United States, Canada, and Australia (3–23). These incursions created declining conditions within each nation's agricultural and trade economies, overwhelmed common people with rising land taxes, and enabled the entry of Western capitalists who worked to recruit cheap labor. By the 1850s, Chinese immigrants began to arrive in Hawaii to labor in the sugar plantations and in California to mine for gold, construct the first transcontinental railroad, gather harvests as migrant farmworkers, and become merchants. Even as Chinese workers were a coveted labor supply for plantation owners and railroad companies, their presence bred resentment among white workers who had to compete against them for work. Such resentment was exacerbated by economic recessions and the completion of the railroad, which brought Americans and European immigrants searching for work. The anti-Chinese immigration exclusion acts of 1882, 1892, 1902, and 1904 represented the cycle of labor recruitment and nativist exclusion that would mark Asian American history (Chan 54–55).

When Chinese immigration was curbed, Japanese immigration was welcomed. When Japanese laborers began to organize in Hawaii, their immigration was restricted by the Gentleman's Agreement in 1907 and an immigration exclusion act in 1924; then Filipino laborers were recruited. Korean and Indian immigrants also entered in smaller numbers but were similarly resented and classed as part of the yellow peril. Chan observes that, even as each ethnic group entered at different stages in U.S. economic development, what they shared contributed to their racialization as a single group: "Asian international migration was part of a larger, global phenomenon: the movement of workers, capital, and technology across national boundaries to enable entrepreneurs to exploit natural resources in more and more parts of the world" (4). Asian Americans, who were racialized in terms of economic threat, subsequently faced economic and political discrimination in the foreign miner's tax, immigration exclusion acts, and alien land acts.

Such anti-Asian discrimination—at times reinforced with violence—constitutes, in Michael Omi and Howard Winant's terms, a series of "racial projects." Race is "a concept which signifies and symbolizes social conflicts and interests by referring to different types of human bodies," but race is slippery as it continues to be rearticulated through "a process of historically situated *projects* in which human bodies and social structures are represented and organized" (Omi and Winant 55–56). According to Chan, racial projects even preceded early Chinese immigration in reports penned by diplomats, missionaries, and merchants whose depictions were inflected by their intolerance of Chinese cultural and economic life (45).

Nativism directed at Asian immigrants on the West Coast and Hawaii was moreover part of the public fever over white identity and American citizenship that followed the Civil War. In *White by Law: The Legal Construction of Race,* Ian Haney López argues that the Civil Rights Act of 1866, which granted birthright citizenship regardless of race, invigorated racism against Asian and Native American persons and new debates over naturalized citizenship. The result: racial projects that took form as fifty-two "racial prerequisite cases" from the 1878 case *In re Ah Yup* through 1952. *In re Ah Yup* is telling, Haney López writes, because it reveals the explicit construction of white and nonwhite identity. In 1878, Circuit Judge Sawyer denied Ah Yup, a Chinese man, the right to U.S. citizenship, reasoning that a Chinese person is not white and therefore could not acquire citizenship. Judge Sawyer employed three lines of argument varyingly invoked in subsequent racial prerequisite cases: "Congressional intent," scientific classification (ethnologists classified Asians as one of five races, different from whites), and common sense (the popular belief that a Chinese person is not white) (Haney López 54).

Later, when scientific evidence contradicted late nineteenth and early twentieth-century common sense—when, for instance, anthropologists claimed that those from India have "Caucasian" heritage—

the courts rejected science and upheld popular belief. Most revealing is Haney López's point that we continue to take race for granted even now; from our vantage point, the court's elaborate reading is "absurd" since we all "know" that a Chinese person is not white: "Accepting the non-Whiteness of Chinese as commonplace truth, we are perplexed and amused by Judge Sawyer's arduous efforts to justify, or rather assert, that same conclusion. The lengthy categorical debates in the prerequisite cases seem ridiculous only because we have fully accepted the categories these cases established. . . . The truly curious, then, is not the typological sophistry of the courts, but our own certainty regarding the obvious validity of the recently fabricated" (55). That is, we bristle at this 1878 case not just because of its overt racism but *also* because we accept racial categories as common sense even now. Common sense hides its own construction. *In re Ah Yup* withheld naturalized citizenship from Chinese immigrants in 1878, *Takao Ozawa v. United States* likewise affected Japanese immigrants in 1922, and *United States v. Bhagat Singh Thind* followed for Indian immigrants in 1923. This was the racial climate that informed Asian American education.

The schools, particularly in communities with significant "Mongolian" presence, were certainly not innocent of racial reasoning that defined the Asian American subject. Because the earliest Chinese immigrants were primarily working-age men, there were few families and thus initially little pressure for Asian American enrollment in the public schools. In fact, the anti-Chinese immigration exclusion acts prompted those who settled in the United States to turn their attention to domestic rights. As Eileen Tamura argues, we currently have very little scholarship on the history of Asian American education ("Asian Americans"), but at least two important studies give us a sense of early Asian American activism for public education in California: Victor Low's *The Unimpressible Race: A Century of Educational Struggle by the Chinese in San Francisco* and Charles Wollenberg's *All Deliberate Speed: Segregation and Exclusion in California Schools, 1855–1975*. An 1855 California school law determined that funds for public education would be distributed based on the number of white children in the state. As early as the 1860s, Chinese immigrants petitioned San Francisco officials for a school where immigrants could learn English, and one school in the city endured openings and closings amid much contention between 1859 and 1871. Only private tutoring, church-based schools, and Chinese language schools were otherwise available to these immigrants until 1885, despite the fact that they paid taxes (Low 13–37).

In 1885, however, Chinese Americans in California did achieve public education. Nine years earlier, *Ward v. Flood* required the state to enroll African American children into the public schools or create segregated schools, particularly in light of the fact that racial minorities were denied access to schools for which they were taxed. The case thus upheld the right of racial minorities to public schooling and strengthened the Chinese American litigation to come. In San Francisco the parents of Mamie Tape, a Chinese American born in the United States, brought suit against Principal Jennie Hurley who had denied Tape admission to Spring Valley School. *Tape v. Hurley* did uphold Tape's right to an education, but in a hurried effort to circumvent the integration of Chinese Americans into white public schools, Superintendent Moulder pushed the legislature to fund what became the Chinese School, later rebuilt as the Oriental School in 1906 (Low 60–70, 92–93; Wollenberg 39–41). While there was pressure for the Japanese to also attend the Oriental School, President Roosevelt needed to intervene as an increasingly powerful Japan protested the discrimination. The Gentleman's Agreement of 1907 halted segregation of Japanese American children, and, in turn, Japan agreed to curb further emigration of laborers to the United States (Wollenberg 54–68).

In the midst of these broad conflicts over racial exclusion and public education, Asian Americans were unwavering in their commitment to language rights and literacy education, seeking to participate in English-speaking business endeavors, support their children's and their own education, preserve ethnic heritage, and bring about social justice. Those early church-based classes in San Francisco, for instance, responded to Chinese immigrants' desire to learn English until *Tape v. Hurley* compelled the school districts to provide public schools for them. The desire for English-language learning, however, was undercut in the territory of Hawaii, where language difference was used to justify separate English Standard schools that effectively segregated white middle-class children from racialized plantation workers' children between 1924 and 1948 (Tamura "The English-Only Effort"; Young "Standard English and Student Bodies").

Racial injury even intruded on the ethnic language schools that Chinese and Japanese immigrants built for their children. Early Chinese immigrants created Chinese language schools that would prepare their children for rigorous academic exams in China because they had been excluded from American schools. Japanese immigrants similarly educated their children in Japanese language schools by drawing on textbooks that taught about Japan's history and culture. By 1920, as the Americanization movement took hold after World War I, a coalition of Japanese language educators decided that the curriculum should encourage the *Nisei* to learn about Japanese heritage and *also* prepare them for life in America. Still, ethnic language schools in California and Hawaii faced mounting accusations of disloyalty to the United

States with perhaps the most vocal opposition in California coming from *Sacramento Bee* newspaper owner V. S. McClatchy (Morimoto 17–31, 55–79). In Hawaii the territorial attorney general Harry Irwin proposed eradicating the schools altogether, but restrictions on teacher certification and curricula were eventually ruled illegal by *Farrington v. Tokushige* (Hawkins). While the internment of Japanese Americans during World War II closed many of these schools, Japanese language schools thrived at the Tule Lake camp, where the "no-no boys" (who refused to sign American loyalty contracts) were largely sent, and then experienced resurgence after the war (Morimoto 117–40).

These histories capture the ways that Asian Americans were denied self-actualization as the good American writing well: those who pursued English language and literacy education had to contend with racial discrimination that prevented them from attending mainstream public schools and limited the resources apportioned to segregated schools, and those who hoped to preserve their family languages were treated with suspicion. Even early arguments for Asian American education hinged on the assumption that Asian Americans were inherently different—namely, depraved and disloyal—and consequently needed an education that would deter them from criminal delinquency. The de jure segregation of the nineteenth and early twentieth centuries gradually receded as Chinese Americans, Japanese Americans, and others of Asian ancestry began trickling into mainstream public schools, and the last racial restriction on naturalized citizenship was lifted in 1952.

At the same time, common-sense notions of race persisted in the more subtle guise of the "model minority," and the achievements of Japanese American students were received warily. In the 1920s and 1930s, for instance, educational researchers drew on intelligence tests to compare white and Japanese American children and found that Japanese Americans scored approximately one grade level lower on the tests but maintained comparable or even higher grades in school (Yoo). While researchers wondered whether language difference might account for the difference in test performance, the discrepancy between test scores and grades was explained by a reaffirmation of standardized tests' objectivity and teacher bias. Furthermore, there emerged an early representation of the model minority as one who works hard but whose native intelligence does not match that of European Americans. The myth of the model minority became firmly entrenched with the publication of William Petersen's 1966 article "Success Story, Japanese American Style" in the *New York Times Magazine* and soon came to signify not just Japanese Americans but more generally the new waves of Asian immigrants who arrived as a result of the 1965 liberalization of immigration policy and the diasporas born of war in Southeast Asia.

Together, the newest immigrants and American-born people of Asian ancestry inherited the promise and denial of language rights and literacy education.

WRITING AGAINST RACIAL INJURY IN THE CIVIL RIGHTS ERA AND BEYOND

For Asian Americans the late 1960s and early 1970s marked a clear turning point in this history of racial formation. Here was a moment when activists from diverse Asian and Pacific Islander ethnic backgrounds organized to interrogate and contend with a history of shared racial othering in the United States. The Asian American movement fostered collective scrutiny of the historical construction of Asian Americans as irredeemable foreigners—whether Mongolian, Oriental, or simply "yellow"—and activists laid claim to a newly politicized Asian American identity (Wei). Such activism was perhaps most apparent in the late 1960s at San Francisco State University, when Asian American student organizations came together with African American, Latino/a, and Native American groups in the Third World Liberation Front (TWLF) strikes and agitated for "self-determination" over their college education. These strikes escalated into a militant stand-off against university presidents, the Board of Trustees, and a governor who saw police force as the antidote to student disruptions.

The TWLF strikes did, in fact, shut down the university and garnered uneasy concessions (including a school of ethnic studies), becoming just one flashpoint to be read in relation to sister protests against institutional racism on university campuses across the country. But as William Wei documents in his invaluable history of the Asian American movement, this growing critical consciousness prompted activism not only on college campuses but also beyond—for example, at the site of ethnic neighborhoods in urban spaces (e.g., Chinatowns) struggling with injustices related to race, labor, and gender. Not surprisingly then, as the racial landscape in America shifted dramatically in the late 1960s and early 1970s, the moment was ripe for Asian American advocacy for language and literacy rights. In the coming years, Asian American activists began advocating for language and literacy and testified to a rising race consciousness through their writing: mission statements and leaflets for student organizations, protest speeches, letters to school administrators and politicians, alternative literary and news publications, and more. Educators and students alike were called upon to nurture home languages, create new forums for writers, and reinvent a public rhetoric that would work toward racial justice.

The educational history of Asian Americans in the United States brings into sharp relief the ways that racial ideologies have shaped our nation's long-standing commitment to language and literacy. Indeed, as Catherine Prendergast explains so lucidly: "If literacy has become the site of struggle for racial justice since the civil rights movement, it is because it has been for so many years the site of racial injustice in America" (*Literacy and Racial Justice* 2). What emerged in the Asian American movement was a recurrent theme in U.S. history: conflicts over language and literacy often masked wider racial tensions. Asian American activism for language and literacy was essentially a struggle to rewrite an educational system long troubled by racial injury and to redefine who can speak and write as an American. As the race-conscious protests of the movement swelled and then settled, Asian Americans faced two pressing imperatives: to reexamine what racial injury meant in present-day language and literacy education and practice, and to adapt their emerging collective rhetoric to changing discourses about race and racial accountability. It is here that my inquiry begins.

This inquiry is informed not only by my position as an educator and researcher interested in literacy studies, ethnographies of communication, linguistic diversity, and ethnic minority rhetorics but also by my background as a second-generation Vietnamese American whose family immigrated to the United States—more specifically, to California—in 1975. For my part, I was introduced to the Asian American movement, the origins of ethnic studies programs, and the idea of race consciousness during my first semester at Berkeley in the early 1990s. My response: uncertainty. On the one hand, I took pride in the Asian American and related race-conscious movements and wanted in earnest to be part of this heritage that belongs to racial minorities in particular and to America in its entirety. On the other hand, I was not sure that I saw myself reflected in this history, partly because I wasn't certain how Southeast Asian refugees fit into this narrative and partly for another reason: the dominant discourse about Asian Americans at the time positioned us as a privileged model minority threatening the white student body on University of California campuses. I didn't feel privileged; I was trying to navigate (and finance) my college education without being privy to the rules of academic life. At the time, I wasn't prepared to reconcile these contradictory racial ideologies.

Close to ten years later, I began to think about the Asian American movement again—this time, as a researcher focused on literacy, language, and ethnic minority rhetorics. Revisiting Wei's historical account of the Asian American movement, I was struck by the role that reading groups, grassroots publications, and other forms of literacy figured into activism at the time. I hoped to study the literacy practices within activist Asian American student organizations and, in doing so, to join scholars who share a curiosity about and engage in ethnographic inquiry into everyday discourse practices of "nonmainstream" communities, to borrow Beverly Moss's phrase (for example, Cushman; Farr; Guerra; Moss *Literacy across Communities* and *Community Text Arises;* Prendergast *Literacy and Racial Justice;* and to an extent, Heath's *Ways with Words,* too). Literacy scholars and sociolinguists who adopt an ethnographic approach seek a thick description of reading, writing, and speaking practices within and across communities. The point of ethnographies of communication, as Dell Hymes's canonical work in sociolinguistics suggests, is to understand the communicative practices within particular communities and, in doing so, generate a map of linguistic practices that emerge not from abstract rules but instead percolate from the ground up in the context of people's everyday lives. Furthermore, such ethnographies may have implications for teaching: "Assumptions are made in educational institutions about the literacy needs of individual students which seem not to be borne out by the students' day-to-day lives," John Szwed contends. "And it is this relationship between school and the outside world that I think must be observed, studied, and highlighted" (Szwed 427).

In light of Asian American and other racial minority student activist calls for "self-determination" over their college education in the late 1960s and early 1970s, it would follow that we ought to critically listen to such activists and identify the rhetorical exigencies "borne out by [their] day-to-day lives." This book argues that we do, in fact, have much to learn from racial minority student activists who have created alternative sites for reading, writing, and speaking: how their speaking and writing positions are informed by racial histories; why and how they speak and write; what conversations call on them to give voice to their concerns and rearticulate their subject positions. As educators, we can then begin to reflect on how these practices might inform our theories, definitions, and curricula about writing and rhetoric.

For these reasons, in 2002, I began my research inquiry with an ethnographic case study of the discourse practices in the Vietnamese American Coalition (VAC), a grassroots college student organization established in 1993. VAC provided a rich research site because of the founding students' mission to incite political awareness and community action. Writing and speech were core to how VAC students invented, extended, and reinvented community—whether in their weekly meetings, mentorship program for local high school students, rallies for political awareness, or relationships with other university and community organizations. In a sense, VAC students faced rhetorical exigencies and employed strategies that echoed activists in the Asian American movement two decades earlier: students sought to understand Asian American subject positions and, through writing and speech, formed community in order to contest and rearticulate what it means to be Asian American. In fact, VAC leaders explicitly recalled their inheritance from the Asian American movement and expressed a desire to emulate earlier activists.

But I also witnessed the kind of uncertainties that, as an undergraduate, I could not name when enrolled in an introductory ethnic studies course. The racial landscape on college campuses and beyond had changed dramatically since the late 1960s. That is, the Asian American movement can be read in the context of what Howard Winant, in *The New Politics of Race*, has described as a post–World War II "global shift" in understandings about race: "Starting after World War II and culminating in the 1960s, there was a global shift, a 'break,' in the worldwide racial system that had endured for centuries. The shift occurred because many challenges to the old forms of racial hierarchy converged after the war: anticolonialism, antiapartheid, worldwide revulsion at fascism, the U.S. civil rights movement, and U.S.-USSR competition in the world's South all called white supremacy into question to an extent unparalleled in modern history. These events and conflicts linked antiracism to democratic political development more strongly than ever before" (xii). Yet by 1970, Winant argues (as he and Michael Omi also argued in their seminal *Racial Formation in the United States*), the response to such activism was marked by "incorporation and containment of the antiracist challenge" (xii). As much as Asian American students in the early 2000s were standing on the shoulders of earlier movement activists, they found themselves in unfamiliar territory, seeking to understand race and contesting racial injury in a culture of postracial discourse. Racial injury lingered by delimiting the subject positions of Asian American speakers and writers; furthermore, student activists had to contend with new demands engendered by a post–civil rights era belief that we somehow had moved beyond race.

As I sought a fuller understanding of VAC student activist discourse practices—interpellations of Asian Americans and writing and speech that affirmed, contested, and/or revised these subject positions—I redefined my research project, juxtaposing my ethnographic perspective with a historical one informed by critical race theory. Put another way, I am still committed to understanding and *recognizing* the discourse practices that govern Asian American student activist communities, but it is only by stripping back layer-by-layer the processes of racial formation that inform Asian American subject positions that we can interrogate why and how Asian Americans are positioned as racial others. With this introductory chapter, I sought to illustrate that American speaking and writing positions have been and continue to be inflected with race and that Asian Americans (and of course, other racial minorities as well as new immigrants) often find themselves confronting this inheritance.

In *Writing against Racial Injury,* I explore Asian American activism for language and literacy in post-1960s California to understand what constituted racial injury and how an emergent Asian American rhetoric attempted to redress such injuries. Drawing on literacy studies, ethnic minority rhetorical scholarship, Asian American studies, and critical race theory, the two parts of this book juxtapose Asian American advocacy for language and literacy rights in the early 1970s and the more hidden and nuanced negotiations of campus racial politics in the early 2000s—two historical counterpoints that more broadly elucidate shifts in race discourse in the post–civil rights era. By examining the shifting politics of Asian American activist rhetorics, my hope is that this study begins to speak into the deep gulf that has long divided histories of language and literacy and histories of Asian Americans in the United States. After all, as LuMing Mao and Morris Young tell us in *Representations: Doing Asian American Rhetoric,* scholars in language, literacy, and rhetorical studies "have seen little work that focuses directly on how Asian Americans use the symbolic resources of language in social, cultural, and political arenas to disrupt and transform the dominant European American discourse and its representations of Asians and Asian Americans" (2). These discursive practices are often what Young has called "minor re/visions," whereby the "minor" works to rewrite mainstream American narratives that have cast ethnic minority practices in shadow (*Minor Re/Visions*). Like Young and the contributors to *Representations,* I hope to build on our understandings of Asian American discourse that reconsiders language and literacy in light of American legacies of racism.

Based on historiography and ethnography, this research project considers Asian American activists who struggled to preserve their linguistic heritage, to authorize their writing, and to fashion an Asian American rhetoric that could respond to contemporary racial politics. To begin, I pose the following questions about the complicated relationship that Asian Americans have with language and literacy education and practice:

In what ways are Asian American speaking and writing subjects already racialized?

Why did language and literacy continue to be contested sites in Asian American movements for racial justice?

How had Asian American student activists engaged in writing and discourse in order to contest and revise their subject positions?

What happened when these revised subject positions interrupted postracial or color-blind discourses?

And finally, how might Asian American activist rhetoric present educators with new and hopeful ways of writing and talking about race in American schools and universities?

Each chapter considers racial injury at the site of language and literacy production. To throw light on the shifts between these two historical counterpoints of the early 1970s and the early 2000s, I have organized the book into two parts: part 1 focuses on Asian American activist rhetoric in the early 1970s, and part 2 looks at the early 2000s.

Part 1 turns first to the 1970s, when activists were harnessing the movement's emerging race consciousness and argued for "self-determination" over their language and literacy education and production. In 1970 the Office for Civil Rights saw fit to name "language minorities" as a group whose civil rights needed to be guarded—a naming act that called attention to the ways language issues had become tropes for racial discrimination. Activism for not only language but also writing was particularly fierce in California, where there were relatively more Asian Americans in public schools and universities. Chapter 1, "Language and Racial Injury in *Lau v. Nichols*," examines the ways that language difference was used to reinscribe racialized subject positions. For several years preceding the 1974 case, Chinese American parents in San Francisco had called on the public schools to provide English language education or, better yet, bilingual education to their non-English-speaking children. When these appeals were denied and when their children's language difference was characterized as deficiency, the parents brought a class action suit on behalf of approximately three thousand Chinese American students against the San Francisco Unified School District, and the case was eventually decided by the Supreme Court. My analysis of *Lau v. Nichols* traces how language difference became the pretext for racial discrimination, arguing that the subsequent unraveling of language rights indicates that the blunt instrument of courts neither exposed racialized understandings of language nor remedied the subtle workings of racial formation. At the same time that Chinese American activists were struggling for self-determination over their children's language education, Asian American activists in universities were demanding self-determination over their writing and writing education.

Chapter 2, "*Gidra* and the Extracurriculum of Asian American Publications," explores the ways activists claimed self-determination by creating alternative forums for public writing. In the aftermath of volatile Third World Liberation Front and other ethnic studies strikes on college campuses in California and across the nation, Asian American and other racial minority student activists continued in their struggles by establishing student organizations and creating alternative news and literary publications. Self-sponsored writing grew out of new Asian American student organizations, and this chapter gives special attention to the student-initiated publication *Gidra,* which would eventually become the ur-text for Asian American student activists. The editors and writers of *Gidra* hoped to create a forum for democratic dialogue, and their writing encouraged them to grapple with their invented ethos as politicized Asian Americans; interestingly, these efforts coincided historically with composition studies' growing concern over nonmainstream students and writing's social function. The chapter explores the ways these alternative student publications register conflict over how to reinvent an Asian American ethos based on an ideology of self-determination, on the one hand, and in response to legacies of racism, on the other. While activism for *Lau v. Nichols* and the publication of *Gidra* addressed different groups and aspects of language and literacy education, both recognized that language and literacy continued to be sites of racial conflict and both had the common goal of self-determination, or the right to direct one's own education. Such activism reflected concerns about racial injury and consequently led to calls for language and literacy rights, whether the right to bilingual education or political voice.

In the next decades, as a *rights* rhetoric came to govern race talk within American education, there were new debates over what constituted racial injury and whose rights should be protected. College campuses saw ethnic studies departments, cross-cultural student organizations, and diversity initiatives more firmly rooted in students' academic and extracurricular lives. At the same time, these commitments to racial awareness also saw intense backlash in light of claims that white students are victims of reverse discrimination and a mounting frustration with multicultural education and political correctness. Many have come to believe that we now live in a postracial state and can return to liberal ideals of colorblind equality. Whereas the 1970s saw Asian American activists critiquing racial injuries that excluded or otherwise constrained their language rights and literacy practices, a younger generation of Asian American activists in the early 2000s found themselves grappling with what Asian American studies scholar Dana Takagi has called the "retreat from race" on college campuses. These activists questioned the ways movement rhetoric might or might not help them figure out how to fight for racial accountability in the present.

Part 2 examines the ways Asian American students drew from their movement inheritance to rearticulate their subject positions and contend with campus racial politics. In particular, these three chapters draw from an ethnographic case study of the Vietnamese American Coalition (VAC), a political student organization in a California university. Based on participant observation during spring 2002, interviews with the twelve most active VAC members and one of the organization's founders, and archived newsletters, this section explores VAC students' political rhetoric and their engagement with campus race talk. Chapter 3, "Campus Racial Politics and a 'Rhetoric of Injury,'" considers the discourses that mediate college students' understandings of race by examining a conflict between "cross-cultural" student organizations and student government leaders who were largely identified as white fraternity and sorority members. The chapter examines the ways the trope of injury mediates racial politics and thereby locks students into perpetrator and victim roles. Underpinning the rhetoric of injury is an ideology of liberal individualism that overshadows social responsibility. Student activists, then, would require alternative rhetorical strategies that recognize our inheritance of racial legacies and work toward reconciliation and an ethic of responsibility.

The next two chapters identify alternative strategies that VAC students used to dismantle reified ideas about race and to redefine an American ethos. Chapter 4, "Asian American Rhetorical Memory, a 'Memory That Is Only Sometimes Our Own,'" explores the rhetorically savvy ways in which cultural memory is used to challenge whose memories are authorized, what gets remembered, and why. I focus here on a VAC student's rhetorical memory as he narrates his protest against Senator John McCain's reference to North Vietnamese "gooks" in the 2000 presidential primaries. In the student's recollections, he works toward what ancient rhetoricians called *copia* and thereby articulates a textured and nuanced notion of Asian American identity.

Chapter 5, "'I WANT A THICKER ACCENT': Revisionary Public Texts," turns to student performances that playfully resignify race and racial accountability. The chapter centers on public texts that reperform Asian American identity: a nonprofit's proposed Vietnamese American studies curriculum, meant to supplement humanities and social science content in the middle schools; a "Culture Night" performance, which one VAC student scripted; and several VAC pieces, including textual art like "I WANT A THICKER ACCENT" and the performance "Speak American Damn It!" Read alongside earlier scholarship in literacy, rhetoric, and composition about ways in which racial minority people "flip the script" (Gilyard *Voices of the Self*; see also Mao; Powell; Schroeder, Fox, and Bizzell; and Villanueva, for example), we see how these performances are instructive to how language and literacy educators might understand the role of discourse in racial formation. Thus, we might arm students with rhetorical strategies that challenge racialized subject positions.

Together, these chapters depict a troubling yet hopeful account of the ways that language and literacy education have alternately racialized Asian Americans while enabling us to rearticulate what it means to speak and write as politicized Asian Americans. It is only through thick description of Asian American activism in the past and present that we can start to appreciate the cultural meaning that language, literacy, and rhetoric have had in their fight for racial justice. Activism for language and literacy rights in the late 1960s and early 1970s was a response to the contradiction between the promise and denial of language and literacy in American history. In their movement for racial justice, Asian Americans worked tenaciously to remedy their exclusion from language and literacy education and production. Close to fifty years later, their legacy remained, but understandings of race and racial accountability were diluted into a rhetoric of injury that tended to emphasize individual rights over social responsibility. By reading closely Asian American activists' powerful and playful rhetoric, however, we are called upon to critically remember our nation's racial legacies and to accordingly reimagine not only an Asian American ethos but also an American one. *Writing against Racial Injury*, I hope, will provide insight to language and literacy educators, historians of education, and Asian American studies scholars who are committed to understanding the ways racial injury shapes our idea of the good American writing well. Asian American activism for language and literacy gives us a glimpse into the ample and diverse ways literacy figured into Asian American cultural production; it also prompts us to rethink the concept of literacy itself and the ways literacy and language are always already inflected with our nation's racial inheritance.

Part 1

Asian American Language and Literacy
Rights in the 1970s

Chapter 1

Language and Racial Injury in *Lau v. Nichols*

The politics of Asian American education since the late 1960s clearly illustrates why we need to deepen our understanding of language heritage and racial difference. Earlier in the civil rights movement, the Supreme Court's 1954 order in *Brown v. Board of Education* that schools desegregate "with all deliberate speed" laid bare the contradiction between racial segregation and American educational ideals. *Brown* was undoubtedly a turning point in struggles for racial justice as the decision not only shaped the social realities of African American and white children but also set in motion widespread scrutiny of injuries of racial exclusion. Yet the problem of racial injury persisted in new guises and even in cases where inclusion was achieved.

"Literacy following *Brown*," as literacy scholar Catherine Prendergast has written in *Literacy and Racial Justice,* "became one of the most prominent battlegrounds on which struggles over what constituted racial discrimination and remedy were fought in the Supreme Court and in communities" (1). In a provocative analysis of Supreme Court cases, critical race narratives, and qualitative literacy studies, she argues that legal and educational discourses have frequently been based on the premise that the right to literacy education is a white privilege. For this reason, efforts to redress racial minority exclusion from literacy education were often read as incursions against whiteness. Prendergast finds that even progressive cases like *Brown* have, in effect, reinscribed whiteness by representing the literacy education provided to white children as the intrinsic standard to which African American children were excluded. Such an assumption preserves the idea of whiteness rather than questioning the systemic racialization of literacy education and American schooling in general.

Nowhere can we see the burden of race on language and literacy education more clearly than in the 1974 landmark case of *Lau v. Nichols,* a class action suit contending that the San Francisco public schools effectively denied close to two thousand students of Chinese ancestry English language instruction (not to mention a curriculum that respected their ethnic heritage) and thus a meaningful education. After years of conflict rife with petitions and ensuing frustration, Chinese American and other civil rights activists grew optimistic when the case was heard and ruled on by the Supreme Court. Justice William Douglas's argument in the majority opinion captures the issue at hand: "Basic English skills are at the very core of what these public schools teach. Imposition of a requirement that, before a child can effectively participate in the educational program, he must already have acquired those basic skills is to make a mockery of public education. We know that those who do not understand English are certain to find their classroom experiences wholly incomprehensible and in no way meaningful." Justice Douglas and his colleagues ordered the San Francisco Unified School District to remedy the problem whether that meant providing English language instruction or a truly bilingual curriculum. The unanimous ruling was momentous for parents, students, and other community members who had fought hard over language minority students' rights, yet the ongoing struggle for bilingual and bicultural education and community activists' demands for a voice in educational matters would continue to face dogged resistance.

The case of *Lau v. Nichols* marks a dramatic recurrence of the nation's contradictory approach to language and literacy education. Why did school administrators decide that the English language education of language minority children fell outside the scope of their responsibility? Why did the courts find that *Brown*'s emphasis on racial justice and equal protection was irrelevant to these language minority students? And how are we to understand the disregard for community activists who sought to remedy this "mockery of public education"? An underlying issue here is that school administrators had cast language difference in terms of ethnicity, not *race*; however, what they failed to recognize was that, by denigrating the ethnolinguistic heritage of language minority children, they were essentially racializing the children. Indeed, language and literacy education was used to mete out racial injury even after the Supreme Court's ruling, and two decades after *Brown, Lau v. Nichols* was a warning for racial justice activists to scrutinize the ways language and literacy would increasingly figure as tropes for race.

RACE, ETHNICITY, AND THE IDEA OF THE (NON-)NATIVE SPEAKER: *LAU V. NICHOLS* IN CONTEXT

Debates over language and literacy are surely no stranger to American politics. These debates have historically called up kindred ones about national unity, American identity, and racial stock (Baker 188–211; Baron, "Federal English"; Crawford; Stevens), and as I have argued, the history of Asian American education bears out the idea that language and literacy education has worked to cultivate the good American writing well while holding this ideal out of reach of racial minority people. What distinguishes *Lau v. Nichols* is that these particular struggles for language minority rights emerged as part of a burgeoning Asian American movement in the late 1960s, which thrust legacies of racism against Asian Americans onto the public stage. Asian American activists, according to William Wei's history of the movement, were inspired by the race-conscious struggles of the previous two decades and more specifically by the Black Power movement.

The movement for Yellow Power began as community and student activists challenged the social and economic plight of Asian Americans living and working in ethnic enclaves, most notably Chinatowns in urban areas. As these activists inquired more deeply into the racial roots of socioeconomic inequities, they critiqued Western imperialism and identified with past and present liberation movements in East and Southeast Asia. The protests against the Vietnam War, Wei suggests, were particularly pivotal in rallying Asian American activists and prompted them to question the racialization of Asian people within and beyond the United States and to fight for social, political, and economic self-determination. It was against this backdrop that Chinese American and other community activists voiced their concerns over the education of non-English-speaking students of Chinese ancestry in San Francisco. Despite this activism for racial justice, it was not always apparent from the *Lau* discourse that language discrimination was inordinately harming racial minorities, particularly Asian Americans and Latino Americans.

L. Ling-Chi Wang, then an activist and graduate student who would later become a notable Asian American studies scholar, has related the struggle in several invaluable accounts ("*Lau v. Nichols:* History"; "*Lau v. Nichols:* The Right"; "Historical Overview"). Parents of language minority children had been troubled for years by the schools' failure to provide their children with a bilingual-bicultural education or even English language instruction. As these children sat in English-only classrooms, they fell behind their classmates, and many of them eventually dropped out of school. Wang takes care to say that litigation was pursued only after many community appeals and only after administrators in the San Francisco public schools addressed language minority students' concerns in pedagogically shallow ways, if at all: "For three years the Chinese-American community held meetings with school administrators at all levels, conducted numerous studies that demonstrated the needs of non-English-speaking children, proposed different approaches to solve the problem, staged demonstrations to protest school indifference and inaction, packed school board meetings to demand bilingual education programs, and developed community alternative programs to rectify the rapidly deteriorating situation" ("Historical Overview" 3).

Not until 1966 did the school district even develop its first formal English language program, a thin forty-minute-per-day pullout session ("*Lau v. Nichols:* History" 59). Parents' requests for bilingual teachers who would provide English language instruction were rejected as many school administrators believed that they were treating all students equally by teaching everyone in the same language: English. School administrators held onto this belief even though the 1968 Bilingual Education Act, or Title VII of the Elementary and Secondary Education Act, began to grant federal funding for the education of language minority students. The San Francisco Unified School District was not unique in this regard: in 1968 none of the Bilingual Education Act's authorized $15 million was distributed, and from 1969 through 1973 "annual funding never exceeded about $35 million even though up to $135 million had been authorized" (Moran 1264–65).

In 1970, Kinney Kinmon Lau and twelve other language minority students, with the support of their parents, brought a class action suit against Alan Nichols, then president of the San Francisco Board of Education. The facts of the case are summarized in the Ninth Circuit Court of Appeals ruling from 1973:

> Two classes of non-English-speaking Chinese pupils are represented in this action. The first class, composed of 1,790 of the 2,856 Chinese-speaking students in the [San Francisco Unified School] District who admittedly need special instruction in English, receive no such help at all. The second class of 1,066 Chinese-speaking students receive compensatory education, 633 on a part-time (one-hour per day) basis, and 433 on a full-time (six hours per day)

basis. Little more than one-third of the 59 teachers involved in providing this special instruction are fluent in both English and Chinese, and both bilingual and English-as-a-Second Language (ESL) methods are used. As of September 1969, there were approximately 100,000 students attending District schools, of which 16,574 were Chinese.

Chinese American and other community activists were understandably frustrated by what they saw as a refusal to treat language minority children fairly. And they were not alone.

When *Lau v. Nichols* was first heard by the federal District Court in Northern California, there was already mounting disillusionment over halting desegregation efforts and resistance against busing programs. The class action suit for language minority students' rights, as many have noted, was clearly related to struggles for equal education in *Brown*. The Office for Civil Rights (OCR) saw fit to remind schools about the importance of Title VI of the Civil Rights Act of 1964; Section 601 of the act reads: "No person in the United States shall, on the ground of race, color, or national origin, be excluded from participation in, be denied the benefits of, or be subjected to discrimination under any program or activity receiving federal financial assistance." On May 25, 1970, Director J. Stanley Pottinger issued a memo that further detailed the act's meaning for language minority students:

1. Where inability to speak and understand the English language excludes national origin-minority group children from effective participation in the educational program offered by a school district, the district must take affirmative steps to rectify the language deficiency in order to open its instructional program to these students.

2. School districts must not assign national origin-minority students to classes for the mentally retarded on the basis of criteria which essentially measure or evaluate English language skills; nor may school districts deny national origin-minority group children access to college preparatory courses on a basis directly related to the failure of the school system to inculcate English language skills.

3. Any ability grouping or tracking system employed by the school system to deal with the special language skill needs of national origin-minority group children must be designed to meet such language skill needs as soon as possible and must not operate as an educational dead-end or permanent track.

4. School districts have the responsibility to adequately notify national origin-minority group parents of school activities which are called to the attention of other parents. Such notice in order to be adequate may have to be provided in a language other than English. (United States Office for Civil Rights)

The memo's emphasis on "national origin" minorities implies that nativism and racism were similarly implicated in discrimination in the schools. Language and other differences marked national origin minorities and thus became sites for injury.

What I find most interesting here is that, even as the memorandum clearly places racial discrimination and national minority origin discrimination in the same class, the Office for Civil Rights leaves hazy the precise relationship between cultural markers of *ethnicity* and the social construction of *race*. Casting these students as "national origin" minorities places emphasis on newcomer status and the different ethnic backgrounds that recent immigrants bring with them. Naming the Chinese American students "national origin minorities" when the Asian American movement was adopting a *race*-conscious identity presented a new quandary in the conflict over language rights. Whereas "ethnicity" can be understood as cultural values and practices (including linguistic ones) passed on and adapted from generation to generation, "race" refers to the differentiation of bodies and cultural heritage where the differentiation leads to hierarchies and oppression among racial groups. Most important, "race" calls up ongoing power struggles, whereby each racial project is "an effort to reorganize and redistribute resources along particular racial lines" (Omi and Winant 56). Casting the students as American racial minorities, by contrast, might have highlighted the ways language discrimination had been deployed as *racial* injury in the United States for more than a century.

The slippage between ethnicity and race also raises difficult questions about how to understand racial injuries against Asian Americans and Latino Americans alongside those of African Americans. After all, the discrimination against language minority students here is undoubtedly reminiscent of the discrimination against dialect difference—specifically, Black English—that sociolinguists had been carefully delineating since the 1960s and 1970s (Dillard; Labov; Smitherman). Dialect difference has been similarly used to relegate African American children to remedial or special education classes, but neither the Office for Civil Rights nor the courts alluded to these shared histories. The elision might be explained by the ways in which different racial groups are understood through the lens of ethnicity. As race theorists Michael Omi and Howard Winant have pointed out, processes of racial formation are often obscured by the "ethnicity paradigm," which essentially likens the experiences of racial minorities to those of white immigrants and encourages minorities to assimilate accordingly (14–23).

This narrow emphasis on ethnicity tends to overlook the legacies of discrimination that thwart assimilation or make assimilation unappealing for those who have been racially differentiated. By conflating "race" with "ethnicity," the ethnicity paradigm fails to account for the social structures that create unfair socioeconomic conditions for racial minorities. Furthermore, the racial construction of blackness is so pervasive that "with rare exceptions, ethnicity theory isn't very interested in ethnicity *among* blacks. . . . It does not consider national origin, religion, language, or cultural differences among blacks, as it does among whites, as sources of ethnicity" (Omi and Winant 22). As a consequence, dialect difference among African Americans is often constructed, in the mainstream, as a marker of racial inferiority and tends not to be recognized as part of one's ethnic heritage. Sociolinguists and African American studies scholars, of course, would contend with these uninformed assumptions. By contrast, because Asian Americans are often constructed as foreigners, their language difference tends to be understood in terms of ethnic heritage from *other* nations and not as a site of racial discrimination within the United States.

To be clear, dialect and language background surely do constitute part of one's ethnic heritage. As feminist and border scholar Gloria Anzaldúa has so gracefully written, "Ethnic identity is twin skin to linguistic identity—I am my language" (59). The problem is that historically this marker of ethnic identity among nonwhite people has been treated as a deficiency and thus has worked to racialize the nonwhite speaker-writer, whether African American, Asian American, Latino American, or Native American. The notion that language marks race is certainly not new. In *Race: The History of an Idea in America*, race theorist Thomas F. Gossett explains that philology in the late eighteenth and nineteenth centuries was used to determine racial distinctions and to develop theories about Aryan linguistic and racial superiority (123–43). The use of language to classify races, of course, did not hold up scientifically. After all, "people who were anthropometrically similar spoke different languages; people who were anthropometrically different spoke the same language or related languages," and the discovery of thousands more languages prompted questions about how many races could exist (125). Still, Gossett posits that these assumptions about race and language persisted within the United States as a preference for Anglo-Saxon language and literature, particularly within university English departments.

Amy A. Zenger's more detailed examination of Harvard's emphasis on English in college writing courses and the students' acquisition of a "mother tongue" corroborates Gossett's claim. By the early twentieth century, the alignment between English and an American subjectivity was further secured with the Americanization movement, the creation of an English language requirement for naturalized citizens, and the federal government's 1919 recommendation that English be the language of instruction in public schools (Baker 190–91). It's worth noting that an appreciation for Anglo-Saxon heritage and the English language is certainly not racist in and of itself; rather, racial injury has arisen when that appreciation was accompanied by an articulation of racial difference and a related denigration of those racial others. In the last few decades, scholars have critiqued the remnants of this ideology in English language education, arguing that the labels of "native" and "nonnative" speakers in schools do not describe a person's language proficiency so much as they reflect idealized notions of who can be "native" (Canagarajah; Leung, Harris, and Rampton; Rampton; Schmidt; Shuck).

Educators working with English language learners might do better to learn from students about their language expertise, affiliation, and inheritance, where "the term *language expertise* refers to how proficient people are in a language; *language affiliation* refers to the attachment or identification they feel for a language whether or not they nominally belong to the social group customarily associated with it; and *language inheritance* refers to the ways in which individuals can be born into a language tradition that is prominent within the family and community setting whether or not they claim expertise in or affiliation to that language" (Leung, Harris, and Rampton 555). Whereas the emphasis on expertise, affiliation, and inheritance calls attention to the experiences of language users, new questions emerge about how these experiences might be shaped not only by individual choice and family background but also by racial politics.

The terms "native" and "nonnative" cue us into the racial ideology that informs language education and policy. In an essay that challenges the assimilationist tenor of the ethnicity paradigm, political scientist Ronald Schmidt has asserted that the establishment of the United States as an English-speaking country has not been racially neutral. Rather, language minorities have often been coerced into assimilating, and "these coercive means of incorporation were accompanied and followed by officially sanctioned social processes of domination and exclusion that were *racializing* in nature, and that included the disparagement of the cultures and languages of these minoritized peoples" (146). As a result, we are left with what second language writing scholar Gail Shuck has called an "*ideology of nativeness,* an Us-versus-Them division of the linguistic world in which native and nonnative speakers of a language are thought to be mutually exclusive, uncontested, identifiable groups"—groups defined by a white "native" identity and its "nonnative" opposite (260).

In short, language education has centered not on the lived experiences of language minority students but on an abstract notion of a native speaker norm that tends to get racialized as "white." Language minority students were not within the San Francisco school board's field of vision as it hired teachers and made curricular decisions. In fact, until the litigation the school district had not even sought to systematically identify how many language minority students might require additional English language education and what their language backgrounds might be. Within this normative language ideology, "nonnative" speakers of English were rendered invisible, so administrators had to rely on teachers' reports, which were not based on an agreed upon definition of language proficiency (Wang, "*Lau v. Nichols:* History of a Struggle" 64 fn83).

These commonplace beliefs about language, ethnicity, and race are important to understand if we are to recognize the *Lau* conflict as a recent episode in the long history of language policy. If school administrators in the San Francisco Unified School District were working from these normative assumptions, it follows that they would see the schools' continued reliance on English-mediated teaching as being fair and even inclusive—primarily because schools had historically disregarded language minority students in their curricula and pedagogical approaches. In their class action suit the appellants in *Lau v. Nichols* began to call attention to racial injustice that resulted from this invisibility. However, the school board sought to distinguish language minority students' concerns from the more public matter of racial discrimination by implying that ethnic difference is a personal matter belonging to individuals.

DENYING RACE: *LAU* IN THE COURTS

Lau and fellow language minority students argued for their right to an equal education within the federal District Court of Northern California in 1970, and the Ninth Circuit Court of Appeals in 1973 before the Supreme Court eventually reached a ruling in 1974. In crafting arguments on behalf of these students, attorney Edward Steinman had to contend with a difficult question: In what ways should the argument for language minority students' rights be aligned with *Brown* and recent legal efforts to remedy racial injury? Put another way, how would they rhetorically address the relationship between struggles for language minority rights and struggles for racial accountability?

On the one hand, there is a simple answer to this question: language policy has undoubtedly played an integral role in the construction of racial difference in American history. Therefore their case could reasonably rely on legal precedent like *Brown* that similarly sought to remedy injustice produced by the public schools. On the other hand, the public was growing unsympathetic toward racial remedies—an aversion that would have tempered the persuasiveness of appeals for racial justice. The backlash against race-consciousness had taken firm hold by the early 1970s, and those who subscribed to normative language ideologies believed that activists who called attention to race, especially to whiteness, were the ones actually *creating* racial strife rather than *responding to* racism. In other words, there was a popular belief that colorblindness would resolve the legacies of racism plaguing American culture. A rhetorical analysis of the arguments in *Lau* reveals that cautious efforts to align language minority students' rights with racial minority struggles for equal education would be met with a denial that race mattered.

The post–civil rights era resistance against racial remedy would have been evident to all parties involved. In fact, the Supreme Court's decision in 1974 begins by nodding toward the California schools' recent desegregation efforts, which resulted from a 1971 federal decree. Attorney Steinman saw *Lau* as the next step in the movement for equal education. At the time, he was a lawyer in the San Francisco Neighborhood Legal Assistance Foundation in Chinatown and had become aware of the ways in which the schools were failing Chinese students in their language education (Euchner). In the early days of community struggle—even before litigation began—it seems that Steinman had already considered the ways in which the hostile racial climate might have affected the case of the language minority students. In the 1994 symposium proceedings *Revisiting the Lau Decision: 20 Years After,* Steinman reflects,

> Why is this case called *Lau v. Nichols* and not *"Gonzalez" v. Nichols?* . . . There are two good reasons why the case was called *Lau:*
>
> 1) It was pure strategy. We thought, "If we win the case, everybody can join us. If we lose, those from non-Chinese communities can blame Steinman and Ling-Chi Wang, and distinguish them from the rest"; and,
>
> 2) It was tactical in terms of the facts. In the late "60s," San Francisco was actually doing a much worse job, percentage wise, for Chinese speaking children than for Spanish speaking children. There were far fewer Chinese speaking children getting anything from the school district, even the one-a-day dosage of ESL. In bringing litigation, attorneys like to present the court with the worst facts because courts may then become most sympathetic.
>
> There was a third private reason, reflected in Ling-Chi's statement about Chinese children being the models—perfect little children. I thought the courts might have an easier time dealing with children from that background than children from Spanish-speaking backgrounds. (6)

Steinman's candid remarks suggest that public sentiment was marked by racial prejudice against Latino Americans, particularly in California, as well as by a widespread misconception that Asian Americans had not endured racial discrimination in the nation's history. In the same years that the Asian American movement was calling attention to Asian American racial formation within the United States, activists' efforts were challenged by the chief narrative circulating about Asian Americans at the time: the myth of the model minority, the "perfect little children."

Just four years before *Lau* was heard by the District Court, the *New York Times Magazine* ran an article that is often cited as being the first to characterize Asian Americans, in this case Japanese Americans, as model minorities. In "Success Story, Japanese-American Style," sociologist William Petersen begins by recognizing the social and economic effects of racism on nonwhite people. He then characterizes Japanese Americans as exceptional minorities who have, through strong character and resolve, achieved the American Dream. Here he invokes the ethnicity paradigm that race scholars like Omi and Winant as well as E. San Juan Jr. have largely challenged: "By any criterion of good citizenship that we choose, the Japanese Americans are better than any other group in our society, including native-born whites. They have established this remarkable record, moreover, by their own almost totally unaided effort. Every attempt to hamper their progress resulted only in enhancing their determination to succeed. Even in a country whose patron saint is the Horatio Alger hero, there is no parallel to this success story" (Petersen 21).

After recognizing the severe discrimination that Japanese Americans had endured through immigration exclusion acts, restrictions on naturalized citizenship, and internment during the Second World War, Petersen goes on to align them with white immigrants who had also faced discrimination. "Yet, in one generation or two," he writes, "each white minority took advantage of the public schools, the free labor market and America's political democracy; it climbed out of the slums, took on better-paying occupations and acquired social respect and dignity" (41). Petersen wonders what distinguishes Japanese Americans from other racial minorities and concludes that they "could climb over the highest barriers our racists were able to fashion in part because of their meaningful links with an alien culture"—unlike the African American person, who "knows no other homeland, who is as thoroughly American as any Daughter of the Revolution, [and therefore] has no refuge when the United States rejects him" (43). The concluding paragraph of the article suggests that Chinese Americans in California might soon follow in the steps of Japanese Americans. For Petersen, the lesson seems to be that the United States had begun to move past race and would continue to do so by embracing a bootstraps sensibility.

Several major news publications—such as *Newsweek, U.S. News and World Report,* and *Time*—echoed the myth of the model minority over the next decades, applying the narrative to other Asian ethnic groups. The myth has been widely critiqued in Asian American studies, not only for denying the heterogeneity of Asian immigrants and relegating racial discrimination to the past (National Commission; Takaki 474–84) but also for pitting Asian Americans against other minorities at a time when pan-racial coalitions were demanding racial accountability. Petersen's praise of Japanese Americans and patronizing sympathy for African Americans perpetuate the racial construction of both groups, inviting readers to blame African Americans for not drawing on their cultures to achieve the "success story" and to consent to the suggestion that Japanese Americans are "alien" and are nowhere near as "thoroughly American as any Daughter of the Revolution." By reaffirming the ethnicity paradigm and its bootstraps sensibility, the myth makes the individual responsible for overcoming social injustices and distracts from the ways in which an uneven playing field has already created inequities along racial lines.

In making strategic use of the "perfect little children" for the sake of language minority rights, Steinman had to work to demand social justice but not deny the racial formation of Asian American students. His remarks reflect an effort to call attention to race *just enough* to make the argument for equal education palatable. On entering the courts, the *Lau* appellants claimed that the San Francisco Unified School District had denied them an equal education through its English-only curriculum, and they based their argument primarily on the equal protection clause of the Fourteenth Amendment and Section 601 of the Civil Rights Act of 1964. These two premises each called up earlier legal efforts to remedy racial injustice. It was during the Reconstruction era that the Fourteenth Amendment became necessary. Once the Civil Rights Act of 1866 granted citizenship rights to those born on American soil (and thus legally enfranchised African Americans), a number of states began to manipulate their laws to deny African Americans equal rights. As a rejoinder, Section 1 of the Fourteenth Amendment provides that "all persons born or naturalized in the United States, and subject to the jurisdiction thereof, are citizens of the United States and of the State wherein they reside. No State shall make or enforce any law which shall abridge the privileges or immunities of citizens of the United States; nor shall any State deprive any person of life, liberty, or property, without due process of law; nor deny to any person within its jurisdiction the equal protection of the laws." This constitutional right essentially forced states to justify differential treatment, particularly uneven treatment of racial groups.

In an article written just before *Lau* reached the Supreme Court, legal scholars Stephen D. Sugarman and Ellen G. Widess explore the equal protection clause argument and explain that differential treatment along racial lines often requires strict scrutiny and must be justified by "a compelling state interest." Furthermore, they elaborate, "a history of invidious treatment of a group, its political impotence and vulnerability, and the inability of a member of the group to free himself of the classifying trait all seem important factors in determining whether or not strict judicial scrutiny is warranted" (163). Sugarman and Widess assert that language minority students do constitute such a group since their language ability "is linked both to their national origin and to their race," even if the schools did not name the students in this way; the school district would thus need to make a case for its interest in an English-only policy (164). The equal protection clause argument was important to the *Brown* decision, and in light of this precedent, many advocates of language minority rights hoped that the courts would likewise affirm this constitutional argument for *Lau* and thereby recognize that language minority students required equal protection.

Brown also figured into the *Lau* plaintiffs' second premise: the Civil Rights Act of 1964 (Gándara, Moran, and Garcia 28). It quickly became apparent that desegregating the public schools with "all deliberate speed" became a vague order that was resisted and only reluctantly implemented. Like the Fourteenth Amendment, the Civil Rights Act of 1964 was passed to redress resistance against *Brown* and broader desegregation efforts and to reaffirm efforts toward racial equality; it essentially guarded against discrimination specifically in social programs receiving federal funding. The act's relevance to language minority rights was further delineated by the Office for Civil Rights 1970 memorandum. According to John Palomino, who helped draft the memorandum, the OCR sought to affirm *Brown* and *Lau*'s shared interest in equal educational opportunity. As a result, "the first draft of the May 25th Memorandum paralleled the Supreme Court's approach in *Brown* by focusing on the exclusion and alienation of being a limited English proficient (LEP) student in America"; later drafts emphasized that this exclusion constituted discrimination against national origin minorities (Affeldt 18).

Even though Steinman did not identify the appellants as *racial* minorities when inside the courts, his argument for language minority students in *Lau* drew heavily from the precedent set by *Brown*. The appellants asserted that English-only education was only a form of "surface equality" because, although language minority students were not physically segregated from the schools, the language of instruction excluded them from the educational opportunity available to other students. In the majority opinion for the Ninth Circuit Court of Appeals, Judge Ozell Miller Trask summarized the appellants' line of reasoning: "As applied to the facts of this case, appellants reason, *Brown* mandates consideration of the student's responses to the teaching provided by his school in determining whether he has been afforded equal educational opportunity. Even though the student is given the same course of instruction as all other school children, he is denied education on 'equal terms' with them if he cannot understand the language of instruction and is, therefore, unable to take as great advantage of his classes as other students." As a consequence, the schools were harming the students psychologically and hampering their academic progress, possibly contributing to higher dropout rates. The equal protection clause would therefore demand that the school board either demonstrate the state's compelling interest in this differential treatment or remedy the inequality.

Even as Trask is ostensibly summarizing the appellants' case, his characterization of their argument points more to the court's and the school board's assumptions about why language minority students were not learning in this educational environment. This explanation emphasizes the responsibility of the language minority student by making the student the subject: "He cannot understand . . . and is therefore unable." Trask releases the schools from any responsibility over the students' failure to learn: "According to appellants, *Brown* requires schools to provide 'equal' opportunities to all, and equality is to be measured not only by what the school offers the child, but by the potential which the child brings to the school. If the student is disadvantaged with respect to his classmates, the school has an affirmative duty to provide him special assistance to overcome his disabilities, whatever the origin of those disabilities may be." The passive phrasing of "if the student is disadvantaged" absents the subject who has produced this disadvantage. Moreover, the issue was not really that equality should "be measured . . . by the potential which the child brings to the school" so much as equality should be measured by the ways in which *the school assesses and responds to* what the child brings to the classroom.

Not surprisingly then, the Ninth Circuit Court of Appeals, affirming the lower court's decision from three years earlier, rejected the language minority students' use of *Brown* as precedent and denied the relevance of the equal protection clause as well as the Civil Rights Act of 1964. In doing so, the courts denied the ways that race had shaped language policy in American history. Trask acknowledges an amicus curiae brief written by the Harvard University Center for Law, which "portrays appellants as 'members of an identifiable racial minority which has historically been discriminated against by state action in the area of education'"; however, he goes on to say that the appellants did not provide evidence of de jure segregation and that "there is no showing that appellants' lingual deficiencies are at all related to any past discrimination." Rather, the majority opinion concludes,

> Every student brings to the starting line of his educational career different advantages and disadvantages caused in part by social, economic, and cultural background, created and continued completely apart from any contribution to the school system. That some of these may be impediments which can be overcome does not amount to a "denial" by the Board of educational opportunities within the meaning of the Fourteenth Amendment should the Board fail to give them special attention, this even though they are characteristic of a particular ethnic group. Before the Board may be found to unconstitutionally deny special remedial attention to such deficiencies there must first be found a constitutional duty to provide them.

The assumption here is that the educational system offers unfettered opportunity to those who are able to overcome their so-called deficiencies. Here again we see the bootstraps sensibility of the ethnicity paradigm, where the "disadvantages" are created by the *language minority*'s "social, economic, and cultural background" rather than by the school that has excluded him or her; in this line of reasoning, it is merely coincidence that these disadvantages are "characteristic of a particular ethnic group."

The court's rationale reflects the public's broader retreat away from race-consciousness and aversion to racial remedy. As blatant racial prejudice became less socially acceptable, ethnic pluralism was often recognized and even affirmed. However, as Schmidt has explained, proponents of a colorblind ideology often assign ethnicity to the private realm of individuals and families, making ethnic difference irrelevant to public policy. That is, "while Americans are free to be as ethnic as they wish, their ethnic diversity must remain a *private* matter, having no legitimate place in the country's public policy" (Schmidt 151). By making ethnic difference a private matter, even well-intentioned advocates of colorblindness were effectively closing their eyes to legacies of racism that had long informed language and literacy education. Schmidt points out that even if racial minorities were fluent in standard English, their assimilation would always be partial since language is only one marker of race.

Language, an aspect of ethnic heritage, was cast not only as a private matter but also as a deficiency in the *Lau* discourse. In the majority opinion, Trask identified the students' language background as "Chinese students' lingual deficiencies," "special deficiencies," "disabilities," "appellants' handicaps," and "disadvantages caused in part by social, economic, and cultural background." The attached clause—"whatever the origin of those disabilities may be"—might be read as a subtle indictment on the families and communities that have apparently caused these deficiencies and allowed them to persist. In a dissenting opinion, Judge Irving Hill also took up the metaphor of "disability" and "deficiency" even as he argued on behalf of the language minority students:

> To ascribe some fault to a grade school child because of his "failing to learn the English language" seems both callous and inaccurate. If anyone can be blamed for the language deficiencies of these children, it is their parents and not the students themselves. Even if the parents can be faulted (and in many cases they cannot, since they themselves are newly arrived in a strange land and in their struggle for survival may have had neither the time nor opportunity to study any English), it is one of the keystones of our culture and our law that the sins of the father are not be visited upon the children.

The majority opinion failed to recognize that the schools were the ones disabling these students. In a dissent to the denied en banc petition (which would have allowed the entire bench rather than a smaller panel to hear *Lau*), Judge Shirley Hufstedler took up the metaphor while critiquing the lower courts' decisions: "Invidious discrimination is not washed away because the able bodied and the paraplegic are given the same state command to walk."

Rather than recognize the ways race has shaped language policy in American history, the Ninth Circuit Court of Appeals affirmed the District Court's decision and rejected the language minority students' petition, in part because they could attribute academic failure not to the schools but to the students' ethnic "deficiencies." Even as both courts "sympath[ized]" with the language minority students, they ruled that the San Francisco school board had provided the students with an equal education by providing them with the same education as others. In other words, the schools were not failing the students so much as the students were failing themselves. When remarking that "the needs of the citizens must be reconciled with the finite resources available to meet those needs," the court implicitly approved of a normative language ideology whereby the school district's finite resources could be distributed based on the idea of the American native speaker.

But *Lau v. Nichols* would be heard one more time, and in 1974 the Supreme Court gave language minority activists reason to celebrate. Most important, the court called up the responsibility that the state of

California had to language minority children and affirmed the legitimacy of remedying the de facto exclusion that the children were experiencing. Writing for the majority, Justice Douglas explained,

> This is a public school system of California and [Section] 71 of the California Education Code states that "English shall be the basic language of instruction in all schools." That section permits a school district to determine "when and under what circumstances instruction may be given bilingually." That section also states as the "policy of the state" to insure "the mastery of English by all pupils in the schools." And bilingual instruction is authorized "to the extent that it does not interfere with the systematic, sequential, and regular instruction of all pupils in the English language."

Because the state made English proficiency a requirement for students seeking a diploma, the public schools had a responsibility to provide instruction that would prepare all students, including language minority students, to meet those standards. As a result, "under these state-imposed standards, there is no equality of treatment merely by providing students with the same facilities, textbooks, teachers, and curriculum; for students who do not understand English are effectively foreclosed from any meaningful education."

Furthermore, even if the school board did not intend to discriminate against these children, the Supreme Court asserted that de facto exclusion on the basis of race or national origin was not legal: "Discrimination is barred which has that effect even though no purposeful design is present: a recipient [of federal funds] 'may not . . . utilize criteria or methods of administration which have the effect of subjecting individuals to discrimination' or have 'the effect of defeating or substantially impairing accomplishment of the objectives of the program as respect individuals of a particular race, color or national origin.'" The recognition of the effects of discrimination—as opposed to discriminatory intent—would be critical to struggles for racial accountability and in fact would soon be heavily contested in legal debates over racial remedy. For the moment, though, the *Lau* decision legitimized the idea that the court could redress discriminatory effects and thus broadened the means by which civil rights activists could legally argue for racial remedy.

On January 21, 1974, the Supreme Court decided in favor of the language minority students, and although they did not identify a violation against the students' constitutional right to equal protection under the law, Justice Douglas and his colleagues did affirm the students' argument based on the Civil Rights Act of 1964 and the related 1970 memorandum. The court thus ordered the school board to redress the unequal education being caused by the English-only curriculum. Declining to intrude on pedagogical decisions, the court enjoined educators to decide on the most appropriate remedy—whether that meant English language instruction or a bilingual-bicultural educational program.

Lau v. Nichols, in spite of the resistance that ensued, was undeniably historic for language minority advocates and civil rights activists in general because it called attention to language discrimination and lent much needed support to arguments for bilingual-bicultural education. Not only did the decision affect about five million students across the nation (Wang "*Lau v. Nichols:* History" 61) but, as legal scholar Rachel Moran has attested, *Lau* inspired Congress to reaffirm the decision with the Equal Educational Opportunities Act of 1974, renew ongoing discussions about amending the Bilingual Education Act of 1968, and create the Office of Bilingual Education (1270–80). Language educators and several legislative representatives, Moran explains, gave strong testimony to the validity and advantages of bilingual-bicultural education. While Congress eventually skirted the question of whether the act meant to encourage English proficiency only or bilingual-bicultural education, the 1974 revision was more open to the latter than the 1968 version had been (1278).

At the same time, *Lau*'s aftermath was contentious. Part of the problem was that the normative language ideology that racialized "native" and "nonnative" speakers of English remained unchallenged. We can see this clearly in the concurring opinion written by Justice Harold Blackmun, who was joined by Justice Douglas: "We may only guess as to why [the language minority students] have had no exposure to English in their preschool years. Earlier generations of American ethnic groups have overcome the language barrier by earnest parental endeavor or by the hard fact of being pushed out of the family or community next and into the realities of broader experience." By comparing racialized language minority students with earlier white ethnic immigrants, these justices reaffirmed the ethnicity paradigm and cued the ways in which the effects of racial discrimination would soon be explained away by the need for family values and community responsibility. In fact, what the *Lau* decision, the Office for Civil Rights, and the Bilingual Education Act all shared was an assumption that the bilingual education programs were "compensatory"—compensating for language minority students' "disabilities." This mind-set bred resentment among those who saw themselves as sacrificing resources for compensatory programs. As Gail Shuck has pointed out: "When educational resources are seen as limited, only the unmarked group's educational possibilities are seen as threatened. If students marked by language background are in a class with 'regular' students, the former are described as having special interests that will impinge on the rights of the otherwise invisible majority" (270).

Language minority activists, by contrast, believed that *all* students would be enriched by a curriculum that would foster bilingual education and learning about diverse cultural heritages. When the San Francisco school board, other local school administrators, parents, and community organizers reconvened to figure out what the *Lau* remedies might look like in the public schools, all parties engaged in a heated struggle over who had the authority to determine the educational goals of language minority students and the district's broader student population. To make matters still more complicated, parents and community organizers found themselves caught in a wider conflict over federal intervention in public schools. In her article "The Politics of Discretion: Federal Intervention in Bilingual Education," Rachel Moran argues that this was the first time in American history that the federal government intervened in curricular matters, which had traditionally been governed by state and local governments. Recognizing that language minority students' needs were not being met, the federal government challenged state and local authority; language minority activists, educational experiences, and English-only proponents also supported a stronger federal role in schooling though each differed in how they envisioned the manner of involvement and its ends. Language minority activists, in particular, believed that the federal government could authorize parents and interested community members, who had a right to participate in educational decision making for their community's children. Despite the frustrations faced by parents and community members, revisiting these struggles can help today's language and literacy educators understand why the goal of "self-determination" had become so central to the Asian American movement and related race-conscious activism.

"Looking to the Bottom": The Importance of Self-Determination in Language Education

Like *Brown v. Board of Education* two decades earlier, *Lau* was met with fierce resistance. But the resistance in *Lau*'s case registered the ways in which civil rights activism for an equal education had actually shifted since the 1954 desegregation order. As Sugarman and Widess put it, "In *Brown v. Board of Education* the Court was concerned with who is allowed in the schoolhouse; in *Lau* the Court is being asked to regulate what goes on inside" (158). Equal education, then, was being redefined not only by inclusion and racial balance but also by curricular policy that would give equal regard to the cultural heritage of diverse students.

Language minority activists asserted that such respect could be fostered by a bilingual-bicultural curriculum, particularly a curriculum that accounted for the voices of parents and community members. For Wang the embittered conflict that followed was therefore twofold, centering on "*who* should be responsible for drawing up the 'appropriate relief' plan mandated by the Court" and "*what* is educationally and legally 'appropriate' and 'effective'" ("*Lau v. Nichols*: History" 62). *Lau*'s aftermath was essentially a struggle over self-determination, or the right of language minority parents to participate in the public schools' educational decision making.

Critical race scholar Derrick A. Bell Jr., in his 1976 essay "Serving Two Masters: Integration Ideals and Client Interests in School Desegregation Litigation," has also noted the ways in which the fight for equal education shifted in the decades after *Brown*: "The great crusade to desegregate the public schools has faltered. There is increasing opposition to desegregation at local and national levels (not all of which can now be simply condemned as 'racist'), while the once-vigorous support of federal courts is on the decline. New barriers have arisen—inflation makes the attainment of racial balance more expensive, the growth of black populations in urban areas renders it more difficult, an increasing number of social science studies question the validity of its educational assumptions" (5).

Indeed, socioeconomic conditions were not good, and neither was the political climate. The recession coupled with a decline in the San Francisco public school population meant that initiating new programs, fighting for busing, and hiring bilingual teachers would be especially difficult. Even the Equal Educational Opportunity Act of 1974, which affirmed the rights of language minority students, was marked by the Nixon administration's rejection of busing efforts. NAACP lawyers, in their idealism, continued to argue for racial balance, Bell contends, and neglected to consider these realities and listen to educators on the ground who felt that struggles for equal education needed to be about more than desegregation. "Racial separation is only the most obvious manifestation of [state-supported racial] subordination. Providing unequal and inadequate school resources and excluding black parents from meaningful participation in school policymaking are at least as damaging to black children as enforced separation" ("Serving Two Masters" 10). Bell advocates for an educational agenda driven by the concerns of educators, parents, and community members who have lived with and experienced the inequalities that activists and federal policy seek to remedy.

The importance of minority experience is posited as a legal philosophy by critical race scholar Mari Matsuda, who proposes that law and justice be determined by "looking to the bottom." Joining her colleagues in critical legal studies and critical race studies, Matsuda challenges the assumptions of neutrality in law, which has historically disregarded the concerns and experiences of racial minorities. The *Lau* conflict exemplifies the ways in which "equal education" was premised on a native speaker norm that excluded language minority students; "equal" clearly did not have the same meaning for all groups. Rather than fall into the trap of utter relativism, however, Matsuda argues that we cannot resign ourselves to skepticism and that our understandings of law and justice ought to be guided by "looking to the bottom," or "adopting the perspective of those who have seen and felt the falsity of the liberal promise" (63). Looking to the bottom requires that we disrupt typical notions of the victim and perpetrator and instead attend to "victim group members" as well as "perpetrator descendants and current beneficiaries of past injustice" (70); this ideology requires deeper inquiry into the effects of racial discrimination across time. She elaborates,

> What is suggested here is not abstract consideration of the least advantaged; the imagination of the academic philosopher cannot create the experience of life on the bottom. . . . The technique of imagining oneself black and poor in some hypothetical world is less effective than studying the actual experiences of black poverty and listening to those who have done so. When notions of right and wrong, justice and injustice, are examined not from an abstract position but from the position of groups who have suffered through history, moral relativism recedes and identifiable normative priorities emerge. This article, then, suggests a new epistemological source for critical scholars: the actual experience, history, culture, and intellectual tradition of people of color in America. (63)

L. Ling-Chi Wang and fellow activists shared this conviction that their "experience, history, culture, and intellectual tradition[s]" could enrich curricular decisions about language education. In deliberating over bilingual education policy, Congress acknowledged the importance of parental involvement in the public schools; at the same time, the role of parents was to be solely advisory, and their authority was thus limited to whatever school administrators would allow (Moran 1279).

In "*Lau v. Nichols*: History of a Struggle for Equal and Quality Education," Wang reflects on the ways that language minority advocates in the community were empowered by their collaborative efforts to generate *Lau* remedies. On February 5, 1974, Eugene Hopp, then president of San Francisco's Board of Education, issued a press release that gave parents and other community members good reason to believe that the school board would encourage their participation in redressing the unequal education that language minority students were experiencing (67). Creating an informed and viable curricular plan became all the more important in light of the increasing number of language minority students in the San Francisco public schools. The overall student population in the school district was declining just as the number of language minority students was increasing (62–63). Moreover, the recent liberalization of immigration policy—and the imminent arrival of Southeast Asian refugees—would only make the need for bilingual education all the more pressing.

Contrary to Hopp's hopeful words, the school administrators' actions suggested that they were not acting in good faith. To begin, their identification of language minority students in the school district seemed questionable. Wang reports that the district identified 5,269 limited English proficient (LEP) students in 1969 and 9,084 in 1973, and there were expectations that these numbers were on the rise. However, in 1974 the number of LEP students identified by the district inexplicably declined to 6,511, according to an April report, and then to 4,911, according to information released in December of that year (63–64). Moreover, in the two months following the *Lau* ruling, the Chinese for Affirmative Action—a well-established community organization focused on civil rights concerns—sent two letters that proposed the creation of a community task force to the Board of Education; both letters went unanswered. Still more frustrating was the fact that the director of Bilingual Education called a meeting on April 15, during which he asked select community members to serve on a Special Advisory Committee and to review and approve his fifty-three-page proposal within eleven days (67–69). For language minority activists, the perception was that the school administrators only wanted nominal participation from the committee.

Frustrated by the board and the superintendent's unwillingness to involve community members in the *Lau* remedies, the Chinese for Affirmative Action responded with the following statements in a press conference:

1. The Board has taken no action and made no plan to effectively meet the mandate of the Supreme Court.

2. The Board, to date, has made no attempt on its own to solicit ideas and concrete proposals from concerned citizens as to how the Board could best meet the mandate of the Court.

3. The Board has so far ignored innovative ideas and concrete proposals from concerned citizens and parent groups.

4. The Board has been deliberately kept ignorant of what its own staff is doing or

not doing and has been effectively shut off from activities at State and Federal levels relative to the *Lau* decision.

5. The Board has failed to comply with a simple State Education Code, requiring the District to conduct annual census of students of limited and non-English-speaking background by April 1 each year.

6. The Board's inaction already has caused the school system to lose a rare opportunity to seek available Federal funds for bilingual education and has placed the District in a position most vulnerable to lose all its existing Federally funded programs due to non-compliance with Title VI of the Civil Rights Act of 1964 and the order of the U.S. Supreme Court. (qtd. in Wang, "*Lau v. Nichols:* History" 69)

Only after the U.S. Department of Justice placed pressure on the board did the board give approval to a Citizens' Task Force and draw on the expertise of the Center for Applied Linguistics (69–70). The task force was comprised of representatives of the major language minority groups in the district (Chinese, Japanese, Filipino, Spanish-surname) as well as representatives delegated by board members; furthermore, the task force invited participation from a teachers' advisory committee (71–72).

The task force was given the charge of composing a master plan to be adopted the next academic year. Drawing from community input as well as from research on language education and information about the San Francisco Unified School District, the group had to decide on the issue circumvented by Congress: Should bilingual education primarily encourage assimilation into English-only classes, or should the schools adopt a truly bilingual-bicultural curriculum for all students? From their collaborative work, the task force created a seven-hundred-page plan that took a strong stance on this question. Wang describes the master plan as follows: "Essentially, the master plan criticizes the existing approaches of the district as 'totally inadequate and ineffective' and calls for a comprehensive, full-time bilingual-bicultural education program of the maintenance type for *all* children of limited English-speaking ability. The plan also invites active participation of English-dominant and English-monolingual students to achieve real integration and to promote peer learning in a truly multi-lingual and multi-cultural setting" ("*Lau v. Nichols:* History" 73). The task force supported the idea that bilingual-bicultural education should be the goal of the master plan, and early in 1975 they received promises from Superintendent Steven Morena that he would present the plan to the Board of Education for consideration.

However, Wang recounts that they soon learned that the superintendent and his deputy, Lane DeLara, who was staunchly opposed to bilingual education, would not present the plan to the board. Neither would they give the task force much needed information from school records in order to fully complete the master plan. Nor would they respond to calls from the task force. DeLara, in fact, presented his own resolution to continue to emphasize English language instruction through an ESL pullout program, to make no administrative changes, to limit the task force to an advisory role, and to only give the issue of bilingual programs further study; the board rejected the resolution ("*Lau v. Nichols:* History" 75–79). In March of 1975, after a series of fits and starts, the board eventually approved a resolution that diluted the task force's master plan but did concede to allowing for bilingual-bicultural education and expanding the school staff and programs (79–80). The approval of the master plan was finally formalized by a consent decree in the District Court in Northern California on October 22, 1976—more than two years after the Supreme Court had ruled on *Lau* and six years after the litigation had begun.

Lau's aftermath illustrates the school administrators' reluctance to create educational policy by looking to the bottom and their tactic of simply ignoring minority concerns and holding fast to a normative language ideology. A year after the *Lau* decision, the San Francisco Unified School District was still spending only 2 percent of its budget to address language minority students—though this was supplemented by newly available state and federal funds (Wang "*Lau v. Nichols:* History" 80). But if Wang's account is a story of frustration, it is *also* an affirmation of the significance of looking to the bottom. The task force's critical engagement in educational matters encouraged cross-cultural exchange among different ethnic groups in San Francisco and helped them determine that a bilingual-bicultural education would best serve their shared values and the student population in their school district.

In 1975 the U.S. Commission on Civil Rights issued a publication entitled *A Better Chance to Learn: Bilingual-Bicultural Education* that also looked to the bottom. Beginning with a brief history of language politics in the United States, the publication moves on to consider the effects of different language education models—namely, an ESL pullout program versus a transitional bilingual program (which *A Better Chance to Learn* calls "bilingual bicultural education"). ESL pullout classes can provide helpful supplemental instruction; however, based on language minority students' testimonies and survey data, the commission found that the English-only instruction given to language minority students during the remainder of the school day largely impeded their progress in most subject areas and left them discouraged and well behind their English-dominant peers. By contrast, "a major aspect of bilingual bicultural education is inclusion in the curriculum of the child's historical, literary, and cultural traditions for purposes of strengthening identity and sense of belonging and for making the instructional program easier to grasp" (U.S. Commission on Civil Rights 29). For this reason the commission recommended that until the students gained facility with English, teachers might draw on the students' native language to facilitate learning in all subjects and to encourage a strong self-concept. Furthermore, *A Better Chance to Learn* asserts that successfully bridging home and school communities "depends greatly on the extent to which parental and community participation is enlisted in design and implementation of the program" (98).

Looking to the bottom, in fact, enabled parents, community organizers, and local schools to see one major concern that Congress only discussed several years later during its 1977 deliberations about the Bilingual Education Act's renewal: the possible conflict between desegregation efforts and bilingual-bicultural education for language minority students. Teaching language minority students in their native languages for part of the day or all day, after all, would have been facilitated by placing children of the same language background in the same classes. As Wang writes, one board member, John Kidder, was initially supportive of the Citizens' Task Force but "was under pressure from advocates of integration who presumed that the bilingual education plan would undermine the already defunct integration program and set up a separate bilingual school system within the SFUSD" ("*Lau v. Nichols:* History" 76 fn82).

The task force's efforts, however, actually embodied the spirit of integration and cross-cultural collaboration; Wang points out that the different ethnic groups had to overcome distrust and work together to reach a consensus about what equal education meant for their children. Their plan did not treat bilingual-bicultural education as compensatory or as a burden on the school district. Rather, they worked toward what disability studies scholars call universal design and envisioned an integrated program where English language instruction for language minorities would facilitate their engagement with classmates and teachers, where English-dominant students would also benefit from learning about languages and cultures, and where hiring additional ESL teachers would not be necessary since assigning bilingual teachers would become part of the schools' norm. "Simple logic requires us to draw the conclusion that," Wang challenges, "if the classrooms occupied by the 6,510 limited English-speaking students were assigned bilingual teachers . . . there would have been no need to have the floating ESL teachers creating an additional financial burden on the school district" ("*Lau v. Nichols:* History" 65). Taken further, looking to the bottom might have sparked much needed community and school discussions about the relationship between dialect and language difference and about what truly constitutes an equal education—a concern relevant to African American and white students as well as to "national origin minority" students.

But the task force had limited influence, and resistance against race consciousness and racial remedy was mounting. Even though more school districts were taking fuller advantage of the higher funding levels of the Bilingual Education Act of 1974 and states and local districts were recognizing more the needs of language minority students, opponents of bilingual education had become more vocal. As Rachel Moran details, when Congress revisited the Bilingual Education Act in 1977, an assessment of bilingual education programs by the American Institute for Research questioned the effectiveness of these programs on the basis of students' English test scores and the length of time that English-proficient language minority students stayed in bilingual-bicultural programs (1284–91). That is, rather than treat these programs as *transitional* bilingual-bicultural education where the end goal is English language acquisition, some schools went so far as to facilitate *comprehensive* bilingual-bicultural education where the end goal is linguistic and cultural diversity. The report was critiqued on methodological grounds and also for reflecting ideological bias (Gándara, Moran, and Garcia 38); however, this assessment, combined with fears that the act could frustrate integration efforts, hurt support for comprehensive bilingual-bicultural education. As a result, the act was amended such that English-speaking students would also be placed in bilingual classes and, in a shift back toward a normative language ideology, "it was far clearer that the primary goal of [bilingual] instruction was English-acquisition" (Moran 1289).

The language minority rights that *Lau* seemed to promise began unraveling more quickly in the next decades, and while it is beyond the scope of this chapter to rehearse the subsequent debates over language policy, it is worth noting that the next years saw a decisive reaffirmation of the native speaker ideal and an ideology of nativeness/nonnativeness. In their article "Legacy of *Brown: Lau* and Language Policy in the United States," scholars Patricia Gándara, Rachel Moran, and Eugene Garcia point to this shift *away* from looking to the bottom:

> Whereas the 1994 version of the Bilingual Education Act included among its goals "developing the English skills and to the extent possible . . . the native-language skills" of English learners, the new law focused only on attainment of "English proficiency." In fact the word *bilingual* had been completely eliminated from the law and from any government office affiliated with the law. A new federal office was created to replace the Office of Bilingual Education and Minority Language Affairs and oversee the provisions of the new law (this is

now the Office of English Language Acquisition, Language Enhancement, and Academic Achievement for Limited-English-Proficient Students, commonly referred to as OELA). What was formerly known as the National Clearinghouse for Bilingual Education—a repository for research on the instruction of English learners—became the National Clearinghouse for English Language Acquisition and Language Instruction Educational Programs. (39)

Moreover, later litigation reversed two important aspects of the *Lau* decision, both of which hindered critical democratic participation on the part of parents and community members. First, the Supreme Court "eliminated private rights of action for disparate impact claims under [Title VI of the Civil Rights Act of 1964], leaving enforcement almost entirely in the hands of executive branch officials" (Gándara, Moran, and Garcia 33). Second, the court increasingly suggested that it would not recognize discriminatory effect and instead would require plaintiffs to prove discriminatory intent.

The emphasis on discriminatory intent and the related disregard for discriminatory effect has been particularly vexing. As critical race scholar Charles R. Lawrence III has argued,

> Traditional notions of intent do not reflect the fact that decisions about racial matters are influenced in large part by factors that can be characterized as neither intentional—in the sense that certain outcomes are self-consciously sought—nor unintentional—in the sense that the outcomes are random, fortuitous, and uninfluenced by the decisionmaker's beliefs, desires, and wishes.
>
> Americans share a common historical and cultural heritage in which racism has played and still plays a dominant role. Because of this shared experience, we also inevitably share many ideas, attitudes, and beliefs that attach significance to an individual's race and induce negative feelings and opinions about nonwhites. To the extent that this cultural belief has influenced all of us, we are all racists. At the same time, most of us are unaware of our racism. We do not recognize the ways in which our cultural experience has influenced our beliefs about race or the occasions on which those beliefs affect our actions. In other words, a large part of the behavior that produces racial discrimination is influenced by unconscious racial motivation. (237)

Put simply, because we have all been acculturated into an ideology shaped by our nation's legacies of racial formation, racial injury can exist even when intent is absent. As a result, by taking no notice of discriminatory effect, the courts can pretend that such racial injury simply does not exist. This emphasis on intent tends to focus on isolated acts rather than the cumulative effects of racial formation. Lawrence proposes that rather than get caught up with questions of intent, our legal system ought to examine a discriminatory act "much like a cultural anthropologist might"—that is, "by considering evidence regarding the historical and social context in which the decision was made and effectuated" (247). Such sociohistorical critique was precisely what language minority activists made evident in their arguments for bilingual-bicultural education.

Language activists and educational researchers had hoped that federal intervention might remedy the injustices happening at the state and local levels. However, this hope was troubled by the fact that English-only advocates were similarly pressing for the federal government to intervene but for different purposes, and even at the federal level prevailing opinions about equal education were turning back toward normative language ideologies. Moreover, as Moran finds, federal intervention hampered the ability of states and local districts to be sensitive to their social, economic, and political conditions. What she suggests instead is that the most effective federal intervention might be an act that more formally authorizes parent and community involvement. Such authority would enable community members a mechanism for calling attention to inequalities, and self-determination over their children's education. If educational matters were decided by looking to the bottom, the federal government could offer civil rights protections and national centers for research and resources; states and local districts could respond to their specific realities; parents and community members could voice their concerns; and all would build a wider base of support for such significant educational reform.

Looking to the Bottom in the Asian American Movement

Language had indeed become a trope for race, and the *Lau* conflict tested civil rights activists who were fighting for equality in the educational system. In 1984, ten years after the Supreme Court's ruling on *Lau, Education Week* revisited the story of this struggle with an article beginning:

> A young graduate of the public-school system here, now a sophomore at the City College of San Francisco, has few memories of his first years of formal education. About all the student, who immigrated to this city from Hong Kong, recalls is that he felt isolated from other students because he could not speak English.
>
> As the years passed, the student gradually learned English. He took Chinese lessons after school for several years, but quit in order to make his English classes a top priority. When he was not in school trying to understand what his English-speaking peers were saying, he watched television for hours on end,

imitating the speech of the actors to eliminate his Chinese accent. "The shows on TV are more or less how the society speaks," he now says.

School officials offered to enroll him in classes for non-English-speaking students, the student recalls, but he told his mother that he would rather learn English without any bilingual instruction. "I said no, because [classmates] said, 'You're an ESL [student]' and laughed at you."

The student, who plans to major in computer electronics at City College, now speaks in a clear voice with hardly a trace of an accent. His name is Kinney Kinmon Lau. He was the plaintiff in *Lau v. Nichols*, the case decided by the U.S. Supreme Court 10 years ago this month that led to an explosive growth in bilingual-education programs here and across the country. (Euchner)

Kinney Kinmon Lau's memory of his early childhood education tells us quite plainly that the judicial and legislative system might help facilitate educational reform, but truly changing the racial ideologies around language would require a major *cultural* shift and a willingness to revise assumptions about language difference as well as "native" and "nonnative" speakers and writers. In fact, in a 2006 assessment of programs for language minority students in San Francisco, a scholar of second language education found that students' needs were still not adequately met due to a shortage of texts and limited opportunities for teachers' professional development on language issues.

Despite the frustrations that Wang and fellow activists faced throughout the *Lau* conflict, their struggles do give us a glimmer of hope. In his accounts of the language minority activist struggles, Wang helps us understand the importance of looking to the bottom, of struggling for self-determination to achieve a racial justice. Indeed, the commitment to self-determination was critical to the wider Asian American movement. By the late 1960s, Asian American activists were growing increasingly disillusioned about the promise of integration and past civil rights struggles. With those promises falling short, the more radical race-conscious activists believed that social justice would only come about through major reforms in social structure and, importantly, with the participation of racial minority people. Whereas Wang and fellow activists worked toward self-determination over language minority students' education, student activists on college campuses were demanding self-determination over their writing and writing education.

Chapter 2

Gidra and the Extracurriculum of Asian American Publications

College students and faculty in the late 1960s and early 1970s were thrust into disorder, where the meaning of American higher education was being challenged and the purpose of college writing contested. The public watched as change swept through U.S. universities: federal legislation sponsored new student financial aid programs and encouraged faculty research; universities grew in size, number, and institutional diversity; the baby-boomer generation enrolled in college; news media worried over a literary "crisis" (again); and struggles for racial justice, women's rights, free speech, and an end to the Vietnam War called up debates over the idea of the university. In California the grassroots Third World Liberation Front (TWLF), a coalition of racial minority student organizations that related to "third world" suffering under imperialism, agitated at San Francisco State College for "self-determination," a separate school of ethnic studies, and open access to their college education. These strikes escalated into a militant standoff against university presidents, a Board of Trustees, and a governor who saw police force as an antidote to student disorder. On December 17, 1968, the *New York Times* reported:

Gov. Ronald Reagan said today that a moment of confrontation had arrived
on California college campuses and that "there is no longer any room for ap-
peasement or give."

The police will ring campuses "if that's what they must do" to keep the
schools running and to protect those who really want an education, the Republican governor told a news conference. . . .

Rather than have the police ringing the campus for months, Mr. Reagan
said, "I would rather suggest concerted plans to get rid of those professors
who've made it apparent that they are more interested in closing the school
than in fulfilling their contracts to teach and, likewise, ridding the campus
of those part-time students or those nonstudents who are the militant leaders
there." ("Reagan Declares")

The reliance on police presence, even after violent clashes among officers and students, only galvanized the resolve of racial minority student activists and convinced others to join strike lines. Rallying cries
of "On strike! Shut it down!" halted business at San Francisco State. In
March 1969 university president S. I. Hayakawa made several uneasy
concessions, including a school of ethnic studies, and the TWLF strike
became a flashpoint for related protests nationwide.

In the aftermath of the TWLF student strikes, racial minority student activists and others in universities faced an uncertain moment.
Here was an uncertainty about the purpose of universities and, more
specifically, college writing. As Irving Halperin, then an English profes-
sor at San Francisco State College, reflected in the *English Journal*: "Later, having left the spectator's sidelines, walking beside striking teachers,
I often wondered how we would be any different once the strike was
over and we returned to campus. After all that had happened, if our
professional and financial losses and investments in the strikes were to
have any worth, then we could not go back to teaching as usual" (1050).
What *would* become of higher education? In what ways would educators and students work toward racial accountability and wider social
justice in universities? For the humanities and social sciences, the era
of civil rights struggles lent new vigor to the social turn in many disciplines, to a critical reconsideration of the social, cultural, and political
implications of intellectual work. Within the field of composition studies, in particular, many educators and researchers saw this moment as
an opportunity to democratize college writing education.

Asian American and fellow racial minority activists were likewise
reimagining the possibilities of university education and created grassroots educational opportunities that fostered political awareness and
writing. As Asian American studies scholar Karen Umemoto writes in
her essay on Asian American activism during the San Francisco State

strikes, "the strike was a redefinition of education, which in turn was linked to a larger redefinition of American society. Activists believed that education should be 'relevant' and serve the needs of their communities, not the corporations" (49). For this reason, student activists at San Francisco State and other universities developed community education programs and, through such programs, learned about local social and economic conditions. Making education socially relevant, however, seemed to run counter to California's 1960 Master Plan in Higher Education. According to Umemoto, the plan—which tiered public higher education into the University of California, California State College, and junior college systems—was tailored in response to business concerns and not in the spirit of community empowerment that student activists were seeking to foster (53–54). With the hope of racial integration wearing off, racial minority student activists increasingly turned to third world nationalisms and sought self-determination. Asian American student organizations—the Intercollegiate Chinese for Social Action, Philippine American Collegiate Endeavor, Asian American Political Alliance—joined African American, Latino American, and Native American student organizations to form the Third World Liberation Front at San Francisco State. Even after the strikes were long over, the TWLF and other coalitions left a legacy of college student groups organized around race consciousness and a related tradition of alternative student presses that sought to foster grassroots education.

Indeed, since the movements for ethnic studies in the late 1960s, Asian American college students have consistently engaged in extracurricular writing that is instructive to how we might understand the purpose of college writing and writing education. Asian American student activists have often seen writing political newletters as a means to grassroots education; the writers and editors themselves, in fact, learned about and questioned the relationship between writing and political engagement. *Gidra*, an Asian American student-initiated newspaper created in 1969, eventually became the ur-text for politicized Asian American student organizations. *Gidra* is instructive in part because its articles document Asian American activists who used writing to claim self-determination in their education, to analyze racial politics, and to participate in cultural production. Their self-sponsored writing not only put into practice composition scholars' now widespread belief that college writing courses should encourage democratic participation in public forums beyond universities but also brings into sharp relief the ways democratic discourses *within* universities often fell short when it came to racial accountability. By considering the extracurriculum of Asian American political publications, I seek to recast and build on composition scholars' efforts to democratize college writing in the years following campus protests for racial justice.

THE EXTRACURRICULUM OF COLLEGE WRITING

The growth of Asian American and other race-conscious student presses can be seen as a relatively recent iteration of "the extracurriculum of composition," an extracurriculum that calls into question the purpose of college writing education. Through a historical exploration of writing groups, composition studies scholar Anne Ruggles Gere has found a long tradition of extracurricular activity in which college students and those outside of the university have engaged in self-sponsored writing education, directly or indirectly challenging the mainstream curricula of undergraduate education. As early as the eighteenth century and on through the nineteenth century, American universities saw the creation of literary societies and debate clubs, where college students composed essays on texts and contemporary issues (Gere, *Writing Groups* 9–31). Literary societies gave students an opportunity to socialize at a time when universities generally neglected student life and also made books available through private libraries and encouraged students to improve in their writing. Weekly exercises included "orations, compositions, forensic debates, disputations, humorous dialogues, essays, or music/drama productions," which were regularly discussed and critiqued (Gere, *Writing Groups* 12).

As educational historian Christopher J. Lucas has described, "literary societies and debating clubs . . . were immensely popular among students of the early nineteenth century, sometimes commanding the fierce loyalties and rivalries later associated only with intercollegiate athletics. In stark contrast with the sterility of classroom exercises, the oratorical and declamatory 'exhibitions' sponsored by literary societies were intellectually robust exercises greatly prized by students. Their entertainment value apart, forensic displays and oratorical contests were regarded as good practice for the sermonizing, teaching, and legal pleading for which students were preparing themselves in their future careers" (130). Student compositions often dealt with political concerns, such as the American Revolution, presidential appointments, and foreign policy (Gere, *Writing Groups* 10).

What this extracurriculum of composition reveals is the substantial contribution that college students have offered (or might have offered) to undergraduate education. "Because they adapted new forms quickly and were closer to the undergraduate pulse than college administrators or faculties," Gere explains, "literary societies had always supplied college curricula with some innovations" (*Writing Groups* 14). Most notably, newly established English departments adopted the pedagogical practices of discussion and critique characteristic of literary societies. Since college courses had already appropriated these approaches to literature, literary societies adapted to stress *writing* more. Writing groups at the time were also proliferating outside of universities—most often in the form of "mutual self-improvement" groups (Gere, *Writing Groups* 32–52). Lyceums, for example, multiplied from one organization to one hundred after two years to three thousand after five years. The peer workshop formats of such writing groups were similarly appropriated by the mainstream curricula, specifically by creative writing and college composition courses.

Even though college students played a critical part in revising writing education in universities, these self-sponsored efforts have largely been cast in shadow as composition studies became professionalized and was framed by disciplinary narratives (Gere, "Kitchen Tables"). For Gere, understanding the extracurriculum of composition is important because such self-sponsored writing asks educators to critically examine traditional approaches to writing education and to foster relationships with communities beyond university walls. She continues, "Our students would benefit if we learned to see them as individuals who seek to write, not be written about, who seek to publish, not be published about, who seek to theorize, not be theorized about" ("Kitchen Tables" 89). Jacqueline Jones Royster and Jean C. Williams have likewise critiqued that composition studies' disciplinary narratives tend to gloss over the part played by actual students, particularly racial minority students (as well as racial minority professionals for that matter) (568). These histories, they stress, have consequences for how we conceptualize college writing and related teacher and student subjects.

The late 1960s through the 1970s saw a parallel effort among students to create an extracurriculum of writing that was not being accommodated by the existing undergraduate curriculum. As racial minority student activists struggled for self-determination in universities across the nation, they formed student organizations and created alternative student presses in order to educate one another and themselves. Even though learning to write more effectively was not necessarily an explicit goal of these groups, writing *was* fundamental to their activism, and many editors and writers saw their publications as being part of their mission to educate readers about racial oppression. Interestingly, it was in the midst of these dramatic movements to democratize university education that the discipline of composition studies experienced a rebirth. College writing courses had already been a core part of American college curricula for more than a century, but the social turn of these decades challenged norms in academic writing and prompted composition faculty to engage in sustained research on the nature of writing and writing pedagogy and to recast writing in social terms. Yet, in reading disciplinary histories, we find that student contributions to and critiques of college writing education are once again hidden. We hardly notice that these decades coincided with a swell in Asian American and other race-conscious activism. We seldom glimpse the rhetoric of Asian American student activists who, at the time, joined racial minority student protests, and we may therefore miss the ways that the students critiqued not only college writing's relevance but also the discourses that shaped racial politics on campus.

Rather, disciplinary narratives tend to emphasize the moment right *after* the protests dissipated. One familiar disciplinary narrative in composition studies goes something like this: the social movements of the 1960s and 1970s catalyzed the social turn in the field. In 1970 the City University of New York adopted an open admissions policy, opened its doors to English language learners, ethnic minorities, and nonmainstream students. Mina P. Shaughnessy, then teaching composition at CUNY's City College campus, would note the mismatch between teachers' expectations and students' writing practices and join those who were rethinking writing pedagogy for nontraditional students. The postmovement university culture, according to Shaughnessy, was one of doubting professors and foundering students:

> Toward the end of the sixties and largely in response to the protests of that decade, many four-year colleges began admitting students who were not by traditional standards ready for college. The numbers of such students varied from college to college as did the commitment to the task of teaching them. In some, the numbers were token; in others, where comprehensive policies of admissions were adopted, the number threatened to "tip" freshman classes in favor of less prepared students. For such colleges, this venture into mass education began abruptly, amidst the misgivings of administrators, who had to guess in the dark about the sorts of programs they ought to plan for the student they had never met, and the reluctancies of teachers, some of whom had already decided that the new students were ineducable. (1)

The CUNY system had begun a new and progressive open admissions policy in 1970, and Shaughnessy's colleagues were disconcerted by the many open admissions students who seemed unprepared for college writing—"strangers" at best. "Most of [these students] had grown up in ethnic or racial enclaves," she explains. "Many had spoken other languages or dialects at home and never reconciled the worlds of home and school, a fact which by now had worked its way deep into their feelings about school and about themselves as students." But the students were not "slow or nonverbal, indifferent to or incapable of academic excellence," Shaughnessy defends; they were "beginners," and by stepping into the "pedagogical West," she sought to explain the logic behind nontraditional students' errors (3–5).

Putting aside the problematic metaphor of the West for now, we might see why Shaughnessy's 1977 book *Errors and Expectations* became central to narratives of composition studies' most recent period. She was dissatisfied with claims of students' inherent deficiency, and she asked why students' writing might differ from teachers' expectations. Shaughnessy was in good company. Since the mid-twentieth century, the stage had been set for the scholar-giants of composition studies who, looking beyond the narrow confines of current traditional rhetoric, were solidifying the foundations for the new research agenda of composition studies: New Rhetoricians who revived the civic orientation of classical rhetoric in college composition; sociolinguists who evidenced the linguistic system of African American English and thus validated language difference; ethnographers of communication who studied living discourse traditions in everyday communities; and professionals who defended against linguistic prejudice with the Conference on College Composition and Communication's position statement, *Students' Right to Their Own Language.* These disciplinary shifts have been important for convincing new generations of composition scholars to explore writing and writing pedagogy as engagement in public forums.

But the story of the emergence of composition studies as a research field is still troubled by a stubborn slippage, an alchemy by which racial minority student activists are alluded to in the "protests of that decade" but then quickly fade into the backdrop. The slippage is so commonplace now that in reading the opening sentence of Shaughnessy's *Errors and Expectations*, the glaring contrast between unnamed racial minority student activists who mobilized university reform, on the one hand, and the open admissions students who seemed so woefully underprepared for academia, on the other, is barely discernible. In fact, Timothy Barnett's archival research at the University of Washington and the University of Michigan suggests that college writing faculty and administrators may have even silenced the contributions of racial minority activists in order to maintain what he has called the "white ground" of English studies.

Shift the disciplinary narrative's focal point, however, and we could just as easily tell a different story about this moment in writing education: one of nonmainstream students who, rather than foundering in classrooms, were fighting for the right to direct their own education. Racial minority student activists at San Francisco State College, Berkeley, the College of San Mateo, City College, Queens College, and other universities delivered protest speeches, wrote letters to fellow activists, launched political periodicals, and generally sponsored their own rhetorical education. Student rallies on the East Coast in 1969 provided the impetus for Shaughnessy's City College faculty senate to support "a separate black and Puerto Rican studies program" and a "new open admissions policy that would stimulate the recruitment of students from poor areas of the city" ("City College"). Composition studies' growth into disciplinarity coincided with perhaps the most transformative era of race-conscious activism in the United States; in disciplinary histories, though, composition scholars' concern for "students who were not by traditional standards ready for college" now seem to overshadow the racial minority student activists' demands for a relevant and participatory English education.

Reading about the open admissions students at CUNY alongside the TWLF activists at San Francisco State, we need to confront the disjuncture between representations of students during this era: between open admissions students who struggled in composition courses and student activists who self-sponsored political publications; between the unknown students in the "pedagogical West" and the TWLF activists who made themselves visible; between students from "ethnic or racial enclaves" who had "never reconciled the worlds of home and school" and the racial minority student activists who held educational institutions responsible for that same failed reconciliation. This is not to suggest of course that representations of racial minority student activists are more accurate than representations of nontraditional students who were unfamiliar with or resistant toward academic writing conventions. Rather, I am interested in racial minority student activists because their self-sponsored writing and their challenges to the university prompt educators to reconsider mainstream composition curricula, to question how students may play a role in their own writing education.

For Asian American student activists in particular, a relevant university education would offer them the opportunity to read about Asian Americans' part in American history, bring their studies to bear on racial and socioeconomic injustices, and participate in rearticulations of American culture. The student strikes and the wider Asian American movement had yielded a critical race consciousness and newly politicized pan-ethnic identity for Asian Americans. The claiming of an Asian American or Asian/Pacific Islander American identity was first a reminder of past racial formations of the Oriental, the Mongolian, and the source of Yellow Peril and second the assertion of a new political subject that disrupted historical racialization. At this time, Asian American political organizations came into view throughout California and across the nation, and each group asserted that the past century of racialization had produced Asian American communities' racial and socioeconomic stratification and that this continued to be neglected by the university and the broader public. Taking a page from Gere, I am interested here in what we can learn from Asian American student publications, an extracurriculum that "is constructed by desire, by the aspirations and imaginations of its participants" and that "posits writing as an action undertaken by motivated individuals who frequently see it as having social and economic consequences" ("Kitchen Tables" 80).

Asian American alternative student presses surfaced when students required forums to write themselves into the curricula and to publicly challenge histories of racialization and ongoing racial injustice. To write ethnic heritage and community politics into histories, to deliver arguments about race in university forums, and to otherwise engage in cultural production: these activities made visible and helped authorize Asian Americans as citizens within society. Perhaps what stands out even more than their speech and writing is the fact that Asian American students and their peers demanded writing forums that would foster understanding of their histories and their present social conditions. The purpose of college writing and university education needed to change such that the curricula would support students' understanding of their cultural histories and foster their participation in society.

Creating *Gidra*: An Ideology of Self-Determination and Yellow Power

It was in the spirit of self-determination that five UCLA undergraduates proposed that the university administration sponsor an Asian American periodical. In 1974 Mike Murase, one of these students, recalls *Gidra*'s origins:

> On the campus of UCLA on the afternoon of February 5, 1969, five students—Dinora Gil, Laura Ho, Tracy Okida, Colin Watanabe and I—met with the administration of the school to discuss the possibility of starting a community-oriented publication which would reflect the sentiments and ideas of the students and the communities from which we came. The rationale was simple: Like the rationale for ethnic studies, we argued that an institution of higher learning has the responsibility of teaching its students not only the ideas of the dominant society but the ideas of many cultures and many histories that make up America as well. We explained to the administration that a forum for discussion of socially relevant topics as well as a vehicle for creative expression was urgently needed in the Asian American community. It was to be an educational experience, we said. The administration didn't buy it, but stood firm on its own proposal to publish a scholarly sociological journal to insure [*sic*]

that a university-sponsored publication would not mar the delicate image of the university.

Later as we sat and talked in the office at Campbell Hall, someone suggested, "Why not start our own paper?" Good idea. But how do we do that? We decided that if each of us contributed $100, it would be more than enough to get started. So it was that five of us, students who had no practical experience in journalism, or for that matter, in anything else, gave birth to the idea that was to become *Gidra*. (34)

The students were skeptical of the university's willingness to change. Murase's implicit analysis was that for university administrators a scholarly journal could effectively respond to the social problems identified by students, but for these activists the product was less important than creating a forum for students to participate in political processes. Writing and publishing were vehicles for self-determination or authority over their education and representation. *Gidra*'s beginnings make visible the boundaries of university education and ask us to re-envision the purpose of writing education. Taking up the spirit of self-determination, these Asian American activists acted on the belief that writing is a means to bridge university life and community engagement, and in their extracurricular pursuits the editorial staff furthered their own rhetorical education during the newspaper's run (from 1969 through 1974).

In April 1969, *Gidra: A Monthly for Asians in America* began to circulate, each copy costing twenty-five cents. *Gidra*'s name aptly symbolizes the newspaper's tone. A monster from the Godzilla movies, the Gidra character nods to the construction of a fierce Asian American activist. But Gidra was also drawn as a cartoon worm with a conical hat on the newspaper's front page, reflecting the occasional self-deprecation or winking tone that accompanied the editorial staff's lack of experience. With both fierceness and humor, the editorial staff ran the first issue. From the start the writers believed that the newspaper ought to encourage democratic dialogue: uncensored expression, critical consciousness of social issues, and no apologies. The editors introduce the paper's vision in the first issue:

Truth is not always pretty, not in this world.

We try hard to keep from hearing about the feelings, concerns, and problems of fellow human beings when it disturbs us, when it makes us feel uneasy.

And too often it is position and power that determine who is heard.

This is why GIDRA was created.

Gidra is dedicated to truth. The honest expression of feeling or opinion, be it profound or profane, innocuous or insulting, from wretched to well-off—that is GIDRA.

GIDRA is TRUTH. ("Gidra")

An editorial note in the October 1969 issue places the paper's idealism in the context of the Asian American movement: "*Gidra* is a student initiated newspaper that attempts to provide a much needed forum for the discussion of the issues confronting individuals of Asian ancestry for contemporary America. It is committed to the exploration of the long neglected history, the heritage and the contemporary problems of the Asian in American society. It is committed to looking inward into the Asian American personality and looking outward to the creation of a more humane society where all men are treated as equals" ("Editorial"). Over the next five years, the writers learned to ask sophisticated questions about the paper's responsiveness to movement goals and its rhetorical effectiveness. Monthly press runs averaged four thousand copies and, in the end, accommodated 247 contributors (Wei 105). Articles shifted in focus from campus politics to an anti–Vietnam War and anti-imperialist stance to final reflections on the movement's lackluster energy, but what remained consistent was a belief that the newspaper was a public forum open to critique and diverse perspectives.

Not surprisingly, *Gidra* was strongly influenced by the TWLF strikes in California and the introduction of a Yellow Power ideology within the wider Asian American movement. Early issues of the newspaper included articles on the rationale for the TWLF strikes at San Francisco State (Kanji) and critiques of university president S. I. Hayakawa, who dismissed *Gidra* as "errant nonsense." Larry Kubota's "Yellow Power!" and Amy Uyematsu's "The Emergence of Yellow Power in America" describe more fully the ideology that informs their writing and activism. For Kubota, "Yellow Power means that we as Asian Americans are seeking greater control over the direction of our lives. It also expresses a determination to effect constructive changes in the larger society. It is not a call for Asians to move out of the mainstream of American life, but instead it says that we should be able to dictate some of the terms of entry into that mainstream" (3). Uyematsu elaborates that the call for Yellow Power was inspired by the Black Power movement and the theories of Frantz Fanon, both of which entail a commitment to challenging U.S. imperialism and capitalism. These dual commitments to third world nationalism and socioeconomic justice are confirmed by Mo Nishida, who reflects on the movement five years after *Gidra* began.

In this sense, *Gidra* typifies the Asian American "alternative cultural site" that cultural studies scholar Lisa Lowe has identified in her oft-cited book *Immigrant Acts: On Asian American Cultural Politics.*

She argues that because Asian Americans have historically been alienated from American citizenship and national culture, there emerged alternative sites for Asian American cultural production, ones "not contained by the narrative of American citizenship" (176). As an alternative cultural site, *Gidra* cues the contradictions of American democratic ideals and the past and present conditions that withhold those ideals from Asian Americans. In struggling against these contradictions, *Gidra*'s editorial staff worked hard to encourage varied and even opposing perspectives at the same time that they were cultivating a shared Asian American ethos.

Media studies scholar Lori Lopez, who places *Gidra* within a long history of ethnic presses, has suggested that ethnic presses will often resist internal criticism in an effort to maintain cultural heritage and values. She finds, however, that *Gidra* as a *radical* ethnic press did indeed make space for productive conflict over what defined Asian American identity. Similarly, *Gidra* writer Steve Tatsukawa places the newspaper in a line of antiestablishment underground presses that began in 1955 and evolved into radical race-conscious publications in the late 1960s, including one released by the Black Panther Party. *Gidra* was thus not alone in its effort to build solidarity among its readers while also inviting critique. As Tatsukawa details: "Within the Asian American communities, publications developed in rapid succession. The Bay Area produced *Rodan, Wei Min, New Dawn, Kalayaan* and *Getting Together. The Asian Family Affair* developed in the Seattle area, and *Tora* in Toronto. On the 'Islands,' *Huli, Working Together* and *Hawaii Pono Journal* were among the leading movement publications. On the East coast, *Yellow Seeds* (Philly) and *Bridge Magazine* (NYC) struggled to make the Asian voice heard. And in Los Angeles *Come-Unity* (Third World), *Chinese Awareness*, and the *Amerasia Journal* joined the pioneer of them all, *Gidra*" (13). In presenting diverse viewpoints, *Gidra* was not hesitant to reveal its ideological conflicts with, for example, the Japanese American newspaper *Rafu Shimpo* and even went so far as to publish harsh letters to the editor that challenged the writers for being too radical or not radical enough.

Still, listening and responding to critique was not easy. Murase tells of ongoing debates among the editorial staff about how much they would edit submitted articles and how they would create a nonhierarchical editing process. Furthermore, during the first year quite a few letters to the editor were critical of the paper's tone, which was sometimes strident and even rash. The most extreme letters were disgusted by the writers' politics, but there were also critiques from readers supportive of the movement—for example, a mother who felt that the swearing made the publication inappropriate for her daughter, a school administrator who felt he had been unfairly represented. The editorial staff seemed reluctant to let go of their assumptions about "truth" and free expression but conceded in an April 1970 editorial that their paper ought to be rhetorically effective:

> GIDRA is one year old this month and it seems appropriate, on this occasion to critically review and evaluate the accomplishments of the past year and to restate the goals and purposes of GIDRA in light of the experience gained.
>
> Our initial objective was to bring about understanding through the exchange of ideas. We felt that any idea or opinion deserved to be heard regardless of the language used. We soon found, however, that people got hung-up on the language and would consequently ignore the ideas expressed. . . .
>
> We had to re-examine our goals and priorities. We wanted to bring about understanding and change, but to do this, there had to be effective communication between all parties. Communication being the precursor to understanding and change, it was decided that the establishment of effective communication had highest priority.
>
> Communication is a give and take process. Each party must be considerate of the other's viewpoint as well as the prevailing customs that govern the communication process. For GIDRA, this meant that four-letter words were to be eliminated whenever it was judged that the message remained essentially unaltered by their deletion. "Movement rhetoric," words like 'exploitation,' 'oppression,' 'imperialism,' and the like, were not to be used unless accompanied by explanations and examples that made their meaning clear. Inflammatory words like 'pig,' 'honky,' were eliminated whenever their use seemed to hinder rather than promote good communication and understanding. ("Editorial" 4)

At the same time, the editors felt that readers also had a responsibility to engage controversial and impassioned perspectives. Neither would the paper strive for objective stories since "an analysis or interpretation of the significance of a particular event will help to tie together seemingly unconnected events and help to establish cause and effect relationships which will hopefully lead to a clearer understanding" (4). Such interpretation would likewise require readers' critical engagement.

Throughout the next five years, *Gidra* remained committed to an ideology of Yellow Power and self-determination and worked on attending to readers' suggestions. Asian American studies scholar William Wei has described these years as being marked by "two perceptible phases": the first was marked by learning how to publish a newspaper and "defining what it meant to be Asian American and involved in the Asian American movement," whereas the second saw the writers address "the antiwar movement, counterculture lifestyles, and radical politics" (106). In the first phase, which was also *Gidra's* first year, the editors primarily considered self-determination in relation to their university education. These issues saw articles on, for example, TWLF and other campus protests, the development of the Asian American Studies Center at UCLA, and the creation of new courses related to Asian American history. *Gidra* staff, alongside other Asian American organizations, were even invited as guest speakers to a course on Asian Americans (Yeh-Lo 6).

After the first year, "*Gidra* gradually changed its focus from the campus to the community, from Asian identity to Asian unity, and from 'what happened' to 'what can we do'" (Murase 36). As *Gidra* turned from campus to community, the editorial staff became particularly passionate about the antiwar movement and third world liberation struggles. The activists' growing interest in more radical perspectives might have been spurred on, in part, by the arrests and suspended prison sentences of three fellow writers who participated in a strike for a campus employee, by the police brutality that two others experienced, and by the May 1970 protests against the U.S. incursion into Cambodia and police violence on several campuses including their own (Murase 36–37). Not only did *Gidra* feature articles on Filipino farmworkers, Japanese internment camps, and the impoverished conditions of Chinatowns, the paper also published stories about the Vietnam War, third world liberation struggles, and the politics of Asian nations. Murase, in fact, found himself in 1971 giving a speech as an American delegate to the Seventeenth World Conference against the A and H Bombs in Japan. These shifts in *Gidra*'s conceptualization of the Asian American movement reflect the writers' emergent construction of an Asian American ethos, a subject position defined not only by racial otherness but also by social responsibility and third world nationalisms.

Beyond the lessons that the writers and editors garnered from publishing *Gidra* each month, Murase tells us that several staff members sought to learn even more:

> Through 1972, we were undergoing more changes, but the most significant was that we began a study group of our own. At our first meeting on April 7, we talked about what we wanted to learn from the study. Evelyn wanted the answer to the question, "How does *Gidra* fit into the overall Movement?" Bruce Iwasaki hungered for "facts—concrete knowledge of concepts like 'imperialism'—some kind of objective body of knowledge." Steve said that "our lifestyles and behavioral patterns are expressions of our ideologies. I want to see how I fit into *Gidra* and the Movement." And so it went. . . .
>
> Finally a study group was organized and here's what we came up with: We would set up study for six week sessions, having a recess and evaluation after

each session, and with rotating chairpersons, and a permanent meeting day, time and place. The study was divided into three parts:

(1) The Objective Conditions—Racism, Sexism, Capitalism, Imperialism . . . and alienation, inequality and irrationality . . . which engenders avarice, individualism, intolerance, irresponsibility, negative self-image and pessimism. We wanted to study Asian American and Third World histories, the War, the institutions in our society, the state of the Movement, etc.

(2) The Goals—Humanism, Socialism . . . ? The examples of the Vietnamese, the People's Republic . . . collectivity, self-respect, self-reliance, self-determination, self-discipline, self-defense.

(3) How to Get from One to the Other, Step by Step . . .

Naturally, it broke down into more manageable sub-categories but that's the rough idea. We read political pamphlets, newspapers, introductory readers, and some "classics." We used different techniques: discussion, investigation, role-playing, autobiographical histories, criticism/self-criticism. (Murase 42)

These writers, through their involvement in the Asian American movement and their production of *Gidra*, grew still more curious about self-determination and liberation struggles. These remarkable efforts to learn about and live according to a new race consciousness are a testament to the resolve of the newspaper's all-volunteer editorial and writing staff. Ongoing study points to the challenges of using writing to rearticulate racial subject positions and to work toward improving Asian American and other disadvantaged communities. Until *Gidra* ceased publication in 1974, the editorial notes continued to raise questions about the difficulties of maintaining a self-sponsored newspaper while remaining committed to movement goals.

RADICAL WRITING? WRITING FOR THE MOVEMENT

As the fifth-anniversary (and final) issue of *Gidra* indicates, Murase and his fellow writers and editors took seriously the rhetorical and political lessons they learned. Several activists who had been with the paper for most, if not all, of the paper's life offer invaluable reflections on what they learned about writing and activism, about "the very subtle relationship between movement and media." The final editorial note in the April 1974 issue of *Gidra* reads:

Left political activity requires participation. Active engagement with people, events and consciousness is the signature of our movement. We've learned that only through practice—seeing and doing—can one truly attain knowledge. . . .

But the most visible aspect of doing a newspaper appears to go the other way. Instead of participating the way everybody else does, *Gidra's* instincts also require the act of observation—recording, preserving, writing it down. On the surface, this looks like non-participation. Even though people on the staff have been active individually or collectively in a wide range of other community movement groups, our reflex to hustle articles and get stuff for the paper can inadvertently cause friction. . . .

Still, it's simply quite important for everyone, especially movement media people, to understand the very subtle relationship between movement and media. ("Editor's Note")

To be sure, it seems contributors to the newspaper would have at least glimpsed the relationship between movement and media along the way. One writer reflects: "By writing about all that is happening, and by presenting a variety of opinions, some type of awareness has to emerge. I felt that, once confronted with what's really going on, people no longer would be able to ignore the conditions surrounding and engulfing us. I know I'm idealistic and I guess I always will be . . . I have to be" (qtd. in Murase 38). The issue in many of these reflections was a rhetorical one and had no easy answers: What role could writing play in political activism?

Gidra was not the only activist organization reflecting on their part in the Asian American movement. As Murase attests, the Asian American youth organization Yellow Brotherhood and the Japanese American Community Services/Asian Involvement organization were also reassessing their work. More broadly, as Asian American studies scholar Glenn Omatsu has discussed when tracing the movement from the 1960s through the 1990s, the mid-1970s marked an era of reversals in race-conscious struggles, reversals that resulted from an economic crisis and a cultural emphasis on corporate interests (88–91). In their article "American Student Activism: The Post-Sixties Transformation," coauthors Philip Altbach and Robert Cohen further delineate that disillusionment with violent protests, a more conservative political climate, and the beginning of the "me-generation," which deterred the same degree of student activism that characterized the 1960s. Still, Altbach and Cohen point out that activism continued in the next decades in different forms and within a less welcoming environment.

In the final issue of *Gidra*, the two articles dealing explicitly with writing and activism—Murase's "Toward Barefoot Journalism" and Bruce Iwasaki's "The Final Venomous Jabberwocky: Feverish Grunts on the Movement and the Word"—hold onto a belief in the value of writing and publishing for activist purposes. Both writers suggest that even as activists should propose structural and material change, they also need to be concerned with cultural production. Iwasaki sums this up by critiquing the binary between, on the one hand, those who believe "words are intellectual bullshit" and, on the other hand, those who believe "the answer lies in words." Writing and composing in different media has clearly shaped our understandings of Asian American identity, of social justice, and of a need for change. For this reason, Iwasaki concludes, "I see part of our role as change agents as, ironically, to preserve history and language. That is, prevent the blocking out of consciousness of America's guilt in Vietnam, or of any other episodes from her genocidal past—including Asian American history. Preserving language means being precise and concrete; exposing Zieglerisms and other evasions by those in power; and appropriating words as socialist weapons by making our communication more participatory, collective, and real" (5).

Iwasaki was concerned that theoretical arguments coming from Marxist and nationalist supporters may have grown dogmatic over the years and thus lost sight of the need for activists to be rhetorically sophisticated in how they communicate their goals. For Murase, too, it seems that the challenge was to persuade readers to become involved in the movement without becoming dogmatic:

> Because the need for institutional changes seems so urgent, we often forget that structural changes alone would not create the kind of world we hope for, that there is also a need to look deep into *our own* souls to expel undesirable attitudes we have artlessly inherited. . . .
>
> Our most urgent task is to build a strong united base, I would think. Then, we must educate with love and understanding; we must be modest and prudent. Such an undertaking necessarily means we must also be willing to learn from people. Can we begin to erase old concepts and strategies to draw closer and closer to the People? Yes . . . easy to say, hard to do. It is true that we have worked with people before; but too often, we have not shown enough love, we have not been persuasive enough, we have turned non-antagonistic differences into antagonistic relationships. We have done it at *Gidra*, both in our pages and in the office. (46)

Together, these reflections point to the ways in which *Gidra*'s writers were working out an Asian American rhetoric.

As LuMing Mao and Morris Young explain, "Asian American rhetoric reflects and responds to existing social and cultural conditions and practices while gathering and disseminating the illocutionary force of past practices. . . . However, as a performative, Asian American rhetoric also actively engages and impacts such conditions and practices" (5). Likewise, Iwasaki and Murase imply that activist writing must recognize histories of racial formation, and *Gidra*'s pieces on Asian American experiences testify not just to a search for personal identity but to a recognition of these histories. The imperative for *Gidra* was to take this further and to persuasively re-perform Asian American as well as the broader American narratives. Writing, they hoped, would then have the "performative force [required to] bring about material and symbolic consequences that in turn destabilize the balance of power and privilege that exists between the majority and minority cultures" (Mao and Young 3). Even as *Gidra*'s final issue questions whether continued publication would achieve this performative force, Murase, Iwasaki, and their colleagues did create a publication that had performative force in terms of inspiring future students to take up where *Gidra* left off. *Gidra* may have ended, but Murase reflects that the editorial staff would continue to explore the ways in which writing could be not just *about* the movement but *for* the movement. He wonders whether *Gidra* might take different forms, such as pamphlets, short position pieces, and so on.

It turns out that in imagining the trajectory of the Asian American movement, Iwasaki was right in saying: "I think . . . that it's time to de-emphasize the facile street rap and charismatic presence in favor of the clarity and style and rigors of written exposition. 1969 is over. Our new propositions must be more subtle, resilient and deep; they won't be things to go shout in the streets" (5). Articulating these subtle propositions would not be simple. For the moment, though, *Gidra* had indeed inspired writers and readers alike to think more deeply about writing and the Asian American movement. Murase sums up:

> As we continue to struggle, what needs remembering now is the richness and vitality of this total experience called *Gidra*, which is much more than just a newspaper. It has been an experience in sharing—in giving and receiving—in a sisterly and brotherly atmosphere. It has meant a chance to express ourselves in a variety of ways. It has been a lesson in humility and perseverance. It has meant working with the people who care about people, and genuinely feeling the strength that can only come out of collective experience.
>
> But what a struggle! (46)

THE LEGACY OF ASIAN AMERICAN PUBLICATIONS, STUDENT ORGANIZATIONS, AND THE MOVEMENT

Published from 1969 through 1974, *Gidra* set the standard for Asian American student publications, eventually leading to calls for a twentieth- and then a thirtieth-anniversary issue. Whether composition scholars were aware of the periodical, *Gidra* and publications like it left a legacy for later racial minority students, a legacy in which writing would be seen as a vehicle for cultivating racial and political awareness. Asian American students' political publications proliferated at many universities. To name a few: at Berkeley, Asian American students produced the *Asian American Political Alliance* newspaper (1969–1970), *Slant* (1991–1997), and *hardboiled* (1997–present); at UCLA, *Gidra* (1969–1974) and *Pacific Ties* (1977–present); at UC Irvine, *East West Ties* (1983–1991), *Rice Paper* (1991–1997), and *Jaded* (2004–2007). By recognizing these Asian American students' extracurricular writing in composition studies' disciplinary narratives, we would be affirming and fostering their self-determination, their right to direct their education and to see writing as social action. As Royster and Williams urge: "History is important not just in terms of who writes it and what gets excluded, but also because history, by the very nature of its inscription as history has social, political, and cultural *consequences*" (563). This is not just about writing a more inclusive narrative of composition studies. The point is to develop a narrative that offers possibility for what writing *could* mean and who writers *could* be.

The extracurriculum of Asian American publications asks us to reconsider whether college writing education might similarly encourage students to use writing to bridge university and community, to generate an invented ethos in response to their racial formation, and to spark new questions and curiosities. A revised disciplinary narrative would also introduce productive subject positions for Asian American writers who wish to intervene in social injustice. *Gidra* began as a way to assert self-determination but concluded with lessons about the rhetorical work involved in cultural production and the need to make connections, to alter subject positions, and to question what role writing has in social processes.

Even though the next decades would bring a political climate that would be more hostile to race-consciousness, the protests for ethnic studies and racial justice on college campuses gifted future generations with cross-cultural student organizations and university commitments to "diversity." As higher education scholar Karen Kurotsuchi Inkelas finds, "participation in ethnic clubs and other diversity-related activities are significantly related to awareness and understanding of Asian American issues and interests. Thus, ethnic club/organization involvement may be a positive influence on APA students' long-term civic and cultural engagement, which would imply that participation in such organizations is important for democratic citizenship" (297). At the same time, these ethnic and racial student organizations as well as wider campus diversity initiatives did not go uncontested. Commitments to diversity and multicultural education, as ethnic studies scholar E.

San Juan Jr. argues, may have recognized higher education's ethnocentric and even racist past; however, diversity initiatives tended to dilute TWLF demands for self-determination into yet another argument for the ethnicity paradigm and each group's struggle to assimilate. Education researcher Peter N. Kiang offers case studies that illustrate how these diluted calls for diversity have affected Asian American youth in one city's high schools, where the principals and teachers tended to see Asian American race consciousness and desires for ethnic student organizations as separatist, as contrary to their sense of racial harmony. As a result, Asian American students' concerns were neglected and teacher-student as well as peer racial discrimination was allowed to persist. By contrast, Kiang writes that an extracurricular opportunity to bring Asian American youth together provided a testament to the self-determination that these students desired:

> When an ad-hoc group of adults and youth first gathered to discuss how community resources could support Asian Pacific American students confronting the issue of racial harassment in school, no one imagined that a few months later, nearly seven hundred young people from more than fifty high schools would attend a Conference for Asian Pacific American Youth (CAPAY). . . .
>
> Although most core members had already been active in their own schools prior to CAPAY, their work on the conference greatly advanced their own leadership skills. Attia, a Pakistani American junior and elected student government head from a suburban school, reflected:
>
>> Organization and leadership—I discovered new ways to think about these qualities. All of us were trying to accomplish the same goal, but in such different ways. We had a lot of conflicting ideas, yet we were good friends. I learned how to be more open and democratic. . . . It really is a process—brainstorming, working with people, putting it on paper, trying it out, implementing it, seeing what happens—that's something really cool that I learned. . . . This was the first big event that I had a real impact on. It's so easy to say, "oh, things will never change," so easy to let all this energy inside me become negative energy. But it's a lot more fun trying to solve things. You can always make things better. (257, 260)

Such opportunities for Asian American and other racial minority engagement in educational decision making would become all the more important in the coming decades.

The ideology of race neutrality and a related turn toward individual interests in the "me-generation" became particularly problematic in light of the post-1965 growth in the Asian American population and the growing numbers of Asian Americans going to college. Since the 1980s, the inclusion of Asian American students had become increasingly complex and contested, especially at universities in California where changing demographics and efforts toward inclusion resulted in majority-minority (primarily Asian and Asian American) student bodies. While Asian American student activists drew on the legacy of TWLF strikes and race-conscious activism, they confronted perceptions that they were overrepresented in California universities. Asian American studies scholar Dana Takagi takes up this issue in her study of the 1980s Asian American admissions controversy at Berkeley. When Asian American studies faculty at Berkeley and Bay Area community members called university administrators' attention to a sudden drop in one year's Asian American undergraduate admissions rates, the terms of debate continually shifted: faculty and community members claimed discrimination against Asian American students; university officials upheld the value of "diversity," which meant higher admission rates of underrepresented minorities; and neoconservative politicians claimed that the drop in Asian American student admission rates indicated reverse discrimination that harmed white and Asian American students. Us-them conflicts became perplexing as different parties resignified Asian American identity through their discourse; a diversity culture as well as the continued representation of Asian American students in California universities helps this complex racial differentiation persist. Asian American student activists, several decades later, were able to draw on resources inherited from earlier activists, but these same activists would find their rhetorical agility tested amid campus cultures of colorblindness.

Part 2

Asian American Rhetorics against Racial Injury in the 2000s

Chapter 3

Campus Racial Politics and a "Rhetoric of Injury"

The prototypical scenario of the privatized response to issues of racial accountability might be imagined as follows:

> *Cain*: Abel's part of town is tough turf.
> *Abel*: It upsets me when you say that; you have never been to my part of town. As a matter of fact, my part of town is a leading supplier of milk and honey.
> *Cain*: The news that I'm upsetting you is too much for me to handle. You were wrong to tell me of your upset because now I'm terribly upset.
> *Abel*: I felt threatened first. Listen to me. Take your distress as a measure of my own and empathize with it. Don't ask me to recant and apologize in order to carry this conversation further.
>
> —PATRICIA J. WILLIAMS, THE ALCHEMY OF RACE AND RIGHTS

> For many students, *diversity* has come to mean nothing more than having readings about oppressed groups "shoved down their throats." . . . This may be the result of too many narratives of the suffering of others, too many annual Martin Luther King editorials, too many ethnic food festivals, too many "No Place for Hate" stickers, too many floor meetings about hate speech in dorms or on Facebook.com, too many Rainbow "safe space" decals, and, dare I say perhaps, maybe, too many multicultural readers.
>
> —MARGARET HIMLEY, "RESPONSE TO PHILLIP P. MARZLUF, 'DIVERSITY WRITING: NATURAL LANGUAGES, AUTHENTIC VOICES'"

It's hard to miss that conversations about race on college campuses are now marked by general weariness and even resentment. Fifty years after the social movements of the 1960s, racial accountability is ordered by what American studies scholar Carl Gutiérrez-Jones terms a "rhetoric of injury." Indeed, injury may be *the* trope by which we understand racial accountability. The trope has clearly been fundamental to identifying and remedying those injuries caused by racial prejudice, but there are also worrisome ways in which the *rhetoric* of injury gets taken up. As educators, we should be troubled by injury's articulations in campus racial politics. We see claims to and refutations against victimization, a desire to occupy injured subject positions, and excessive attention to individual distress and anxiety. We live in a privatized system that scrutinizes so very closely the wounds of individuals that it deflects critical attention from the material conditions, cultural systems, and histories that produced racial injustice in the first place. And according to feminist historian Joan W. Scott, "the way to make a claim or to justify one's protest against perceived mistreatment these days is to take on the mantle of the victim" (17). How did victimhood become so sought after, seemingly *desirable*?

What concerns me most about this cultural logic are the ways that democratic discourses intending to make right past racial injustices have made appeals to injury desirable. If language and literacy educators are committed to fostering student expression in public forums generally and university communities specifically, we need to question systems of racial accountability that jerk students into discursive subject positions defined by victim-aggressor relationships. Whereas part 1 of this book examined Asian American activism around language and literacy education in the late 1960s and early 1970s, part 2 looks at the ways in which Asian American activists' rhetoric was tested by diversity discourse by the beginning of the twenty-first century. Diversity discourse, in a twist, had come to advocate for racial inclusion and *also* to undermine those same struggles. Part 2 draws from a 2002 ethnographic case study that reveals the ways in which such diversity discourse impacted a grassroots student organization, the Vietnamese American Coalition (VAC), whose members were committed to building solidarity with fellow college students, younger and older Vietnamese generations, and the local ethnic enclave. In their belief in solidarity and coalition building, VAC was standing on the shoulders of earlier Asian American activists who struggled for self-determination.

Yet the emphasis on solidarity and a related social responsibility needed to be adapted in response to a rhetoric of racial injury. The idea of a rhetoric of injury offers significant explanatory power for composition scholars' multivalent critiques of multiculturalism, diversity, and colorblindness. A rhetoric of injury can fuel the reification of racial categories, the dissipation of these categories into an "absent presence" (Prendergast "Race"), and the difficulties of college students' "diversity fatigue" (Himley 451). This chapter draws on Gutiérrez-Jones's notion of a rhetoric of injury to help us understand anew earlier investigations into race and discourse in composition studies; next we examine the ways in which VAC students addressed a rhetoric of injury in a race-inflected student conflict. VAC students' capable reasoning, their recasting of *ethos*, and their general frustration call attention to difficulties arising from a rhetoric of injury. This rhetoric of injury was informed by liberal assumptions; the students were hopeful that justice could be attained by the individual, often cast as a freedom-fighter type. But the blame game of injury and a related faith in the *individual* stymied a deliberation over *community* values related to racial accountability. Despite such frustrations, these students' rhetorical strategies also provide points of departure that allow us to reimagine a productive conversation about campus racial politics.

In language and literacy scholars' commitment to democracy, where the response to racial legacies is now understood through the trope of injury, we can take care to foster students' understanding of the historical production of racial difference, its impact on speaking/writing positions, and the ways in which difference is rearticulated in the present. Whether through administrative policy or curricular content, diversity discourse in this post-1960s era is an institutional performance of racial difference, and the unhappy epigraphs at the outset of this chapter tell us quite plainly that we have much work to do in delineating the ways public institutions continue to mediate America's vexed history of racialization. As VAC students joined earlier efforts to engage in self-determination, their efforts were tested by the ways diversity discourse hailed them into speaking and writing positions defined by injury.

"To Come Together and Create a Movement": VAC's Beginnings

When I asked one student activist in the Vietnamese American Coalition in 2002 what he hoped fellow VAC students would work toward in the present and the future, he was clear and definitive: "To come together and create a movement." Despite diversity within the student organization, the VAC students I interviewed in 2002 all agreed that this was one of their primary aims. This statement, however, could have just as easily described VAC's beginnings nine years earlier.

On February 11, 1993, two undergraduate students at a southern California public university, cofounded the Vietnamese American Coalition. At the time, these students were writing for the political news magazine of an Asian Pacific American student organization, trying to, in one cofounder's words, "get the word out, get people angry, and get people involved." Envisioning new connections among Vietnamese American students and the local Vietnamese community, the two writers believed that their fellow Vietnamese American students needed not only to celebrate ethnic heritage but also to adopt an activist stance. VAC quickly became a grassroots college student organization, created by and for students committed to community activism—activism that reflected their positions as Vietnamese Americans, as students at this university, and as people with deep allegiances to a Vietnamese diasporic community. "We are a new organization," began the first issue of the *VAC Newsletter*, "seeking members with a strong desire to not only learn about the issues pertaining to Vietnamese people, but to also play an active role in shaping the future of the Vietnamese American community."

During Asian American Heritage Week that spring, the newly formed VAC joined other Asian American student activists to demand that the university administration fulfill earlier promises of a fully developed Asian American studies program, as opposed to the nominal program then in place. "Asian American Studies NOW!" student activists insisted. Students had grown frustrated with painfully scarce Asian American studies course offerings and faculty. The *VAC Newsletter* reported that in addition to a hunger strike and other protests that week, "over 300 students, staff, and faculty as well as community members stormed the administration building, climbed five flights of stairs, and occupied the Chancellor's Office and corridor for over three hours." These students held the university accountable to a two-year-old promise to develop ethnic studies programs. The newsletter further explained:

> In 1991, after several mass protests organized by the Ethnic Students Coalition Against Prejudicial Education (ESCAPE), the administration promised to meet ESCAPE's demands, the most pressing of which was to establish ethnic studies programs. Today [in 1993], programs for African American Studies, Chicano/Latino Studies, and Native American Studies have been developed, while the Asian/Pacific American student population remains without a studies program of its own. Asian/Pacific American students constitute the largest ethnic group on . . . campus with 43.4 percent of the undergraduate population, but their demands have not been met. Currently, only two courses dealing with Asian American issues are offered regularly at [the university]. The demand for these two classes is so great that the waiting lists of students who want to enroll regularly exceed 400. In addition, the only faculty member who specifically researches Asian American issues has received offers from several other universities. Students believe that the administration has not made a concerted effort to hire and retain the qualified professors necessary to develop an Asian American Studies program.

Students' demands for four new faculty positions and their desire to have a voice in Asian American studies curricula may not have been met immediately, but these protests led to important talks among students and administration. These students indeed came together and created a movement. I call attention to the statement "to come together and create a movement" not only because it characterizes VAC's past but also because this was articulated in 2002 in reference to VAC's present and future. The recurrent desire for solidarity (to come together) and activism (to create a movement) should not necessarily be read as a critique that earlier cohorts had failed to achieve a "movement," but rather as a testament to the idea that "movement," as a process of political engagement, never ends.

In 2002 I sought to learn about their movement rhetoric through an ethnographic case study. In the spring quarter, I was an active participant and observer of weekly general meetings, cabinet meetings, and social events. I participated in VAC's mentorship program in which I mentored two high school students, and I also attended a variety of events: postmeeting dinners in the local Vietnamese enclave; a weekend picnic for mentors and mentees; a student government meeting; a trip to see the movie *Y Tú Mamá También*; a showing of the documentary *Who Killed Vincent Chin?*; an Asian American community organization's curriculum press release and hate crime discussions; a Culture Night performance; and the VAC end-of-the-year banquet. To complement participant observation, I researched VAC documents housed in the library's university archive and conducted interviews that extended through the summer of 2002. Archival documents included most issues of the *VAC Newsletter*, the VAC constitution, brochures, flyers, correspondence regarding Vietnamese language courses at local colleges, and more. Lastly, I interviewed the twelve most active 2001–2002 students, two alumni, and VAC's staff adviser (also the head librarian of the archive); pseudonyms are used for all individuals. These students took great pride in VAC's past and present, and they believed that the story of VAC's student community and its activism should be read.

WORKING TOWARD SOLIDARITY: VAC's GROWTH AS AN ACTIVIST STUDENT ORGANIZATION

To understand VAC's engagement in the conflict addressed here, it's important that we first consider the organization's mission and changing perspectives. In the first issue of the *VAC Newsletter*, the cofounders articulated their mission:

STATEMENT OF PURPOSE

The purpose of the Vietnamese American Coalition . . . is to promote active involvement and to voice issues pertaining to the Vietnamese American community, as well as addressing social and political concerns relevant to Vietnam.

1. Campus/Organizational Objective

    a. Seek committed volunteers interested and concerned with the Vietnamese community.
    b. Raise awareness toward Vietnamese student issues.
    c. Be a representative voice of the Vietnamese student population.
    d. Network with existing Vietnamese and Asian organizations, both at [the university] and other campuses.
    e. Develop leadership skills toward group and community participation.
    f. Raise sufficient funds for VAC's functional purposes.
    g. Produce a monthly newsletter to address issues.

2. Community Objective

    a. Form a bond between students and the general Vietnamese community.
    b. Promote awareness of issues relevant to the Vietnamese community.
    c. Handle problems that have arisen and implement programs to prevent ones that may arise in the future.
    d. Communicate with community organizations.

3. Vietnam Objective

    a. Act as a forum to promote awareness and exchange ideas concerning Vietnam.
    b. Be active and responsive to potential issues relating to Vietnam by publicly addressing our collective opinions.
    c. Develop relationships with community leaders and representatives.

The threefold purpose to participate in activism at the levels of university, "Community," and "Vietnam" reveals students' *multiple* positions. VAC students at this time embraced their responsibilities as students, as members of a Vietnamese American diaspora, and as people of Vietnamese heritage. Here, we see evidence of double, even multiple, consciousness.

For Vietnamese Americans, the desire for solidarity and activism can be traced to both a fragmented ethnic identity and a fragmented racial identity. First, like other diasporas, Vietnamese communities in the United States have experienced a sense of alienation and loss of ethnic heritage. VAC students' parents and/or students themselves emigrated under the traumatic circumstances of the Vietnam War. In the first wave of immigration following Saigon's fall on April 30, 1975, 130,000 Vietnamese refugees came to the United States, through four major refugee camps, including Camp Pendleton in Southern California (Zhou and Bankston 9). Between 1975 and 2000 the Vietnamese population in the United States swelled from 15,000 to more than 1.1 million people. More locally, VAC students in 2002 were part of a large community of Vietnamese and Vietnamese Americans in Southern California.

As Vietnamese communities in the United States grew, a densely populated Vietnamese cultural and commercial center developed into the "community" with whom VAC students hoped to form close bonds. The growth of the local Vietnamese community increasingly revealed a disjuncture between 1.5 and second-generation Vietnamese Americans on the one hand and their first-generation parents on the other. Vietnamese American writer Andrew Lam captures this sentiment of loss in a story centered on April 30, the day that the Vietnamese American diaspora treats as a memorial but that Vietnam calls National Liberation Day: "'April 30, 1975?' said Bobby To, my 22-year-old cousin in San Francisco. 'I don't know that date. I don't remember Vietnam at all.' April 29, 1992, is more meaningful to him, Bobby said. 'It's when the race riots broke out all over our country. To me it's more realistic to worry about what's going on over here than there.'" As 1.5 and second-generation Vietnamese, VAC students recognized the fissures in their community and understandably began a movement toward solidarity in the United States. Fighting for social justice, the younger generation worked to make sense of their parents' Vietnamese heritage, their own Vietnamese American experiences, and the dominant American culture.

Not only did their fragmented ethnic heritage foster the desire to come together, but VAC students' *racial* identities as Vietnamese *Americans*, part of the "yellow" race, also contributed to demands for solidarity and activism. For VAC students, racial identifications were specific to U.S. sociopolitical histories, where students identified with American racial struggles. Like the character Bobby To in Lam's "Goodbye, Saigon, Finally," many children of first-generation Vietnamese identify as much with racial struggles in the United States—for instance, with the Los Angeles race riots resulting from the acquittal of four police officers who beat Rodney King—as with their parents' allegiances to Vietnam. As racial minorities, Vietnamese American narratives are interwoven into the history of racial injustices in the United States, specifically the "yellow peril" that depicts Asian Americans alternatively as a threat or as a model minority.

Negative representations of Vietnamese American heritage in both educational curricula and popular media have led to a disjuncture of self and public perception. Vietnamese American studies scholar Linda Võ Trinh describes the thorny double consciousness that results:

In response to my ethnicity, I often hear some variation of "I served in Viet-nam" or "Where's the best pho restaurant in town?" or "I have this wonderful Vietnamese girl who does my nails." I know that I am not the only one to hear these comments or questions, although I have had to learn not to take offense, especially when they come from strangers trying to initiate polite conversa-tion. In my gracious moments, I think at least Americans are not just associ-ating us only with that war in which we were perceived as helpless peasants, barbaric warriors, or cheap prostitutes. But nowadays our ubiquitous soup joints have influenced culinary taste, and our interactions are amicable, even if it is only while we are servicing their beauty needs. Currently, with the US and British invasion of Iraq, I hear the term "Vietnam War" in the media con-stantly; however, the reference is rarely about the Vietnamese or Vietnamese Americans. I am troubled by the parameters of these perceptions about us. (ix)

Attending a university with a majority Asian American student pop-ulation, VAC students attempted to make sense of their double con-sciousness. A majority-minority campus, the undergraduate popu-lation in the fall of 2001 was 2 percent African American/Black, 47 percent Asian/Pacific Islander, 8 percent Chicano/Latino, 26 percent White/Caucasian, and less than 1 percent American Indian; 14 percent are not known. Seven percent of the students in the spring of 2002 were Vietnamese. One student wrote in the newsletter:

As I developed friendships with other Vietnamese students, I gradually began to feel more comfortable as a Vietnamese as well as an Asian. . . . The most noticeable change was that my memories of Vietnam and of the journey to the United States were revived. When I had told stories of these memories to my Caucasian friends in high school, these stories were looked upon with curios-ity; as if they had come from a strange and distant world. And so each time I spoke of these memories, they became more like someone else's stories. I was growing distant to my roots.

The writer concluded that her participation in VAC and other activist student groups enabled her to reject her self-othering and to come to grips with her racial identity. Like Võ, VAC students were also "trou-bled by the parameters of these perceptions about us" and soon gath-ered the impetus for a movement toward solidarity.

Early Activist Years, 1993–1994

VAC's movement toward solidarity included complex and even com-peting ways of working toward solidarity. That solidarity took the form of student activism and coalition building with other student groups is not surprising. Student activists, in their 1993 movement for an Asian American studies program at the university, stood on the shoulders of the 1960s student activists who changed the face of U.S. universities by demanding ethnic studies programs. The introduction of the movement for ethnic studies programs catalyzed the use of coalition-building forces and, as a result, such activism did not end in the 1960s but echoed throughout U.S. universities for decades. One important difference, however, was that this later generation benefited from the institutionalization of earlier Third World Liberation Front (TWLF) movements, including cross-cultural student organizations, ethnic studies courses (even if limited in number), and university commitments to diversity. Early VAC activism often worked from *within* the institution.

Students at the university in 1993 wanted an education that reflected the cultural memories of the majority Asian American student population, and because so many years had passed since the 1960s social movements, the fight for Asian American studies felt particularly urgent. In the 1990s Asian American studies was scarcely present in the university, so VAC students and fellow activists felt a need to voice their concerns. The university soon scheduled more Asian American studies as well as Vietnamese language courses, the latter offered through the continuing education program.

To discuss and plan such campus-wide activism, VAC students early on developed two forums to exchange ideas and to set plans in motion: meetings and newsletters. VAC developed a cabinet that was initially made up of a chair and vice chair but later expanded to include specific program directors, a newsletter editor, a freshman representative, and a board of advisers (including alumni and community members); a librarian in one of the university's archives, Helen, served as their staff adviser. Each week, two meetings were held: cabinet meetings and general member meetings. Both Michael, one of VAC's cofounders, and Bryan, the 2001–2002 VAC chair, described the cabinet as having a facilitating role. In practice, officers and general members alike jointly raised issues, voiced opinions, and made decisions. This forum has been one of the most consistent features of VAC since it was founded.

In addition to meetings, newsletters also became a forum for students to address issues pertaining to the university, the local Vietnamese community, and Vietnam. The *VAC Newsletter* seemed like a logical next step for VAC's two cofounders, who had been writing for another student organization's Asian Pacific American news magazine. With Helen as their adviser, VAC was fortunate to have their newsletter and other literature documented in the university's library. Reviewing the archival documents, I found that year-to-year changes in the topics of newsletter articles corresponded to the changing politicization in VAC that alumni and 2002 students reported. Newsletters therefore documented the history of VAC's events and students' concerns.

In the early years the newsletter often began with an introduction to the organization, the front matter being informative for new and returning students. A narrative of VAC's beginnings and its "Statement of Purpose," for instance, grace the front page of the inaugural issue. Reviewing the first two volumes of newsletters, readers find articles addressing a variety of local political issues: the struggle for an Asian American studies program; a Vietnamese American student conference held at UCLA; and an announcement for a conference on AIDS. We also find topics that broaden VAC's civic and political identifications: an article condemning the incident of hate crime against Loc Minh Truong in Laguna Beach; a letter to a city councilperson and congressperson critiquing their proposal to deport immigrants convicted of gang-related crimes; position pieces on religious freedom in Vietnam and Clinton's lifting the trade embargo; reflections on gender; film reviews and critiques; and more. These newsletters became a forum for students' reflections on all three elements of their commitment: university, community, and Vietnam.

As newsletters and VAC's early activism suggest, the early years of VAC's history showed expectations for political activism and what became challenges to the university to respond to Vietnamese American students' needs. Students also began to build early relationships with community organizations. In 1993 they started to work with a well-established Vietnamese nonprofit organization, tutoring recent Amerasian immigrants from Vietnam. In recounting how he cofounded VAC, Michael wove the making of the student organization into a larger fabric of Asian American activism on campus: "So in the winter of 1993. That's when we started. And at the same time, it was—I think it was a time where a lot of students were beginning to get involved in a lot of Asian American issues on campus." From the start, VAC activism was focused on revising the undergraduate curricula to reflect Asian American heritage. Students set out to change university praxis and start up connections with local community leaders and organizations.

Shifting Political Commitments, 1994–1997

In the academic years 1994 through 1997, VAC students continued on the same political trajectory, and it was not long before they extended their political activism and adopted new interests. Alison, an alumna from this period, remarked on VAC's seeming lack of direction during these years. As both Michael and Bryan commented, the goals of VAC seemed more difficult to locate as the years went on. Still, VAC students managed to turn their attention beyond university walls to issues of representation and treatment of Vietnamese and Vietnamese Americans. In 1995 students critiqued the representations of Vietnamese men and women in the Broadway play *Miss Saigon*, specifically arguing against Vietnamese women's continual roles as prostitutes and helpless victims in films, dramas, and other fiction. The protest initiated an explicit critique of historical representations of Vietnamese, more generally Asian, women—a critique echoed in newsletter articles that celebrated International Women's Day, narrated personal experiences with sexism among Vietnamese Americans, negotiated American and Vietnamese ideals of womanhood, and critiqued popular war films like *Heaven and Earth*.

In addition to this awareness of ethnic gender representations, students turned their attention to local, national, and transnational sites. During this period another student humanitarian group committed to refugee detainees was in the process of folding. Alison, a leader in this student group, explained that she and others had given their support to Vietnamese refugees who were being detained in the Whitehead Detention Camp in Hong Kong—petitioning on their behalf and writing letters to them. The refugee camp shut down in the mid-1990s after the refugees' forced repatriation and the student humanitarian group dismantled.

During this period of transition, Alison became involved in VAC. Not surprisingly, her field of vision extended beyond the university. In 1996, Alison and other VAC students boycotted Nike products and protested in front of a nearby Niketown store, making known their unwillingness to tolerate Nike's abuse of Southeast Asian labor. A local paper reported on VAC and other activists: "Outraged by reports that female workers who make the sports shoes in Vietnam are being exploited, the students are organizing a demonstration at Nike Town at Triangle Square on Saturday afternoon. Protesters are calling for a boycott, and they are organizing a letter-writing campaign, not just to Nike founder Phil Knight (the sixth-richest man in America, according to CBS News), but also to the US Congress." In terms of local community involvement, students continued to build connections with Vietnamese and Vietnamese American community members. This period saw the birth of the Vietnamese American Mentorship Program (VAMP); Shadow Day, an annual one-day event where college students host high school students in a day in the life of an undergraduate; the annual "Little Saigon Clean-up," where students and other volunteers clear litter from the streets; and an increased effort to build partnerships with community members.

As the scope of VAC's activism widened, the newsletter experienced a different shift, from local civic and national political issues to more personal writing and program announcements. After the two cofounders graduated, a new cohort of students began contributing articles to the *VAC Newsletter*. Newsletters continued to feature occasional political articles (e.g., on immigration legislation) and informative program announcements, but writers turned to cultural articles on such topics as reflections on gender and gender representation, personal narratives about being a Vietnamese American student, and film reviews. The 1995–1996 issues, in particular, reflect the most marked shift as the newsletter's title changes from issue to issue, each named after a popular Vietnamese dish (e.g., the *Chả Giò* and *Bánh Bột Lọc*). These issues, moreover, devoted the most attention to expressivist forms through fiction and poetry, a logo contest, and personal messages.

VAC's ongoing activism and the newsletter thus indicated a potential shift in or broadening of interests, critiqued by several members and alumni as a lack of direction. The challenge for VAC students, which became more of a challenge in the coming years, was to clarify VAC's goals: to return to VAC's original vision of political grassroots activism; to embrace students' attraction to cultural and social events by merging with another Vietnamese student organization with these interests; *or* to redefine VAC's changing or diversifying aims.

Redefining VAC's Activist Origins, 1997–2002

In the years before I first became acquainted with VAC students in 2002, they continued to confront this challenge even as they maintained the activities and events that had been established in previous years. The newsletter production was reduced from once every two months to quarterly, and by 2001 the newsletter was no longer produced. Rather, individual students often e-mailed short announcements of upcoming events and forwarded messages about political issues to a list of current members, potentially interested students, and some alumni. Writing was no longer a collective activity; VAC's organizing primarily took place orally through meetings with one another and with other partners. Students solidified and began new informal partnerships with other student groups; during spring quarter of 2002, when high school mentorship funding was threatened, VAC identified their interests with Japanese American, Asian Pacific American, Latino/Chicano, and African American student groups.

The continuation of long-standing activities like meetings, the high school mentorship program, Shadow Day, the Little Saigon Clean-up, and the end-of-the-year banquets attest to VAC's firm place in the university as a student organization, but these programs also indicate that VAC was firmly part of the institution, and students' responsibilities to sustain long-standing programs did not leave them time to initiate new programs. VAC's difficulties in returning to grassroots activism were partly a bittersweet consequence of having achieved institutional status. With a small number of students (who had full course loads, part-time jobs, extracurricular commitments, and family obligations) orchestrating these events, new initiatives was challenging.

Still, in the last five years of the period examined, student activism occurred unpredictably, although its documentation is limited because the newsletter was no longer being produced. Later cohorts of students were able to benefit from the curricular initiatives taken in 1993 and thereby learned about histories of Asian American activism. Several students in the spring of 2002 had taken or were then taking courses addressing Asian American history or other issues. Two students that quarter, Duc and Bryan, wrote research essays on Asian American movements—respectively, on women of color in women's movements and on the growth of ethnic studies curricula in universities. Such coursework prepared students to place their activism in a historical context. In terms of the grassroots organizing characteristic of VAC's early years, according to VAC's staff adviser Helen, Duc received his fifteen minutes of fame on CNN and MSNBC during a protest in Little Saigon. Duc led fellow VAC and other Asian American activists in a protest, which chapter 4 explores, against Senator John McCain for McCain's unapologetic use of the racial epithet "gook" during his 2002 presidential campaign. In the spring quarter of 2002, Duc led a protest against the university for removing free-speech kiosks, and VAC's cabinet challenged the undergraduate student government's curtailment of high school mentorship funding.

Interestingly, in these later more institutionalized years, although VAC sometimes received criticism for its flagging political action, I interpret their movement as changing in nature. Early movements toward solidarity and activism had been predicated on models of U.S. social movements—that is, coalition building for a political purpose that often challenged institutions and individuals in power. Students identified with one another through such political issues, which touched on race/ethnicity, gender, civil rights, and labor. In VAC's more recent history, however, student activism seemed to emerge more out of individual initiative and sometimes showed more play with rhetorical conventions. This shift to personal writing and individual initiative seems related, at least in part, to several members' interests in expressivist creative writing and individuals' rights to voice their political views. Both the individual initiative and rhetorical play, I believe, required a great amount of energy and creativity.

Take, for instance, two ways in which VAC's community activism changed, which I discuss further in chapter 5. First, alumni and students began working from within institutions. Michael argued that we need to make a place for Vietnamese American history and issues in K–12 curricula. After graduating from the university in 1994, Michael persisted in activism—first earning a master's degree in public policy from Harvard, then cofounding the Orange County Asian Pacific Islander Community Alliance (OCAPICA), a nonprofit organization with an operating budget of more than a million dollars. At the time of our conversation in 2002, he was working for a foundation as a grant maker.

Concerned with what youth learn about Vietnamese Americans, Michael and an OCAPICA project team created a Vietnamese American social science and humanities curriculum, meant to be integrated into mainstream high school coursework. Several members of the team describe the development of the curriculum:

> The study of Vietnamese Americans, in particular, is limited to the study of the Vietnam War in US history classes. There is a lack of historical awareness about Vietnamese Americans within US society, other than broad media images of the "natives" of the Vietnam War. Familiar cultural stereotypes and gender representations include sadistic Viet Cong soldiers, helpless villagers, and desperate prostitutes. Since 1975, Hollywood films and videos have run the gamut of Vietnam War storylines. After an initial silence in the years immediately following the war, we saw plotlines about the returning soldier and his confrontations with the family, with the nation, and with himself. Later, we saw films about adopted Vietnamese immigrant children learning their ABCs and becoming "model minorities," and storylines that concluded with reparations for Agent Orange disasters and post-traumatic stress syndrome. Our youth, seeing these one-dimensional images and hearing only bits of their parents' experiences, need a better understanding of the historical and political contexts of the war, of the emigration of Vietnamese from their homeland, and of the formation of new Vietnamese communities in the United States and elsewhere. (Beevi, Lam, and Matsuda 167)

This absence of Vietnamese American history from youth education became a catalyst for the OCAPICA curriculum, which includes the following sections: a historical overview, timelines, maps and demographics, lesson plans, primary sources, a glossary, a bibliography, other resources, and a list of project committee members. With the press release of the curriculum in April 2002 and its pilot implementation into one local high school district, the curriculum's authors point to schools as a potential resource for reviving Vietnamese American collective memories. Two VAC students, Duc and Bryan, interned at OC-APICA, both wanting to reclaim Vietnamese American cultural memories and both perceiving the public school system as one avenue.

Also working to change institutions from within, VAC alumna Alison, after graduating in 1999, spent her spare time working with the Union of Vietnamese Student Associations. The Vietnamese Student Association (VSA) is a student organization at many universities across the nation. VSA students celebrate culture through performances and organize social events for fellow VSA members. As part of the Union of VSAs, Alison helped to organize annual Tết, or Vietnamese Lunar New Year, community celebrations.

Changes in VAC's community activism are evident in a second set of events that embraced play with rhetorical conventions. This play heightened involvement from audiences and performed solidarity. In June 2002 two VAC students, Mai and Duc performed "Speak American Damn It!" in a student-produced performance art show. The performance played with Vietnamese and "American" languages to suggest a performative understanding of "American"—that is, we construct America through our everyday actions. Earlier that year, also in the fine arts corner of campus, VAC student Son posted flyers around campus that stated "I LOVE YOUR ACCENT" and "I WANT A THICKER ACCENT," making a commentary on the rhetorical and aesthetic effects of accents. Both Mai and Duc's performance art and Son's textual art played with what we typically understand to be activism, an argument with premises often taking the form of protests, petitions, or formal speeches.

When I last spent time with VAC students in the summer of 2002, VAC's future was uncertain: full of possibilities but also full of challenges to define and act on a vision that students deemed meaningful. Students had hopes—in some cases, competing hopes—for more members, more political activism, more leadership from the cabinet to make that activism happen, and more leadership from the general membership. In these hopes there remained a sense that movements toward solidarity and activism that had occurred in the past, as varied as they were, would likely take new shape in the future.

AVAILABLE SUBJECT POSITIONS: WHAT DOES DIVERSITY ASK STUDENTS TO BECOME?

By 2002, VAC's desire "to come together and create a movement" was in tension with the racial landscape on many college campuses. Since the 1960s, demands for racial minority self-determination were facing resistance from those who recognized past racism but who argued for colorblindness on campus. Advocates of race neutrality have often claimed that race consciousness in the present constitutes its own form of racism, or reverse discrimination. In these decades, those who argued for the continued importance of race consciousness *and* those who advocated race neutrality found that their discourse was shaped by the idea of injury, where racial injustices constitute violations "against the 'jur,' against the law, rights and accepted privilege" (Gutiérrez-Jones 24). American studies scholar Carl Gutiérrez-Jones's *Critical Race Narratives: A Study of Race, Rhetoric, and Injury* explicates a "rhetoric of injury" that typically operates under an assumption of moral equivalences, balancing the effects of victimization against perpetrator responsibility. To be emphasized is his claim that injury is not simply determined through the authority of legal institutions; rather, injury is moreover "continually rearticulated and jostled as it is employed in a rhetorical battle," a matter of composition and interpretation (25).

Compositionist Phillip P. Marzluf's essay "Diversity Writing: Natural Language, Authentic Voices" speaks to the impact of this injury culture on higher education and gives special attention to the college composition teacher's role. In a piece that is generally supportive of the trend to merge diversity general education requirements and composition courses, he cautions that "diversity writing" risks calling on students to perform authentic voices and on teachers to be "saviors" who expect true-to-self writing. A more critical curriculum would reject authentic conceptions of voice and teach students to recognize how they personally "participate in diversity as a social system" (519). Marzluf's critique is revealing because the salvationist impulse among some teachers is not only the counterpart to a minority student needing salvation; the savior suggests a *triangular* relationship with the presumed victim, who has either been denied her or his authentic linguistic heritage or is ignorant of it, and the injurer, who is responsible for the exclusionary act. With diversity writing at the nexus of savior, victim, and injurer, students have few productive subject positions from which to write—especially if the student is cast as one who injures himself or herself. Indeed, what *does* diversity ask us to become?

To get beyond this problem, we need to step back to figure where our cultural *systems* have led us away from a productive sense of racial accountability. Whereas Marzluf continues to find hope in the "personal," compositionist Margaret Himley's response to his essay challenges that composition pedagogy must venture farther from the personal—from the belief in "a stable self in need of greater audience awareness" (450)— and toward promoting ethical relationships within an "economy of affect" (456). The current economy, after all, has yielded this:

The word diversity makes me a little sick, too. Its problematic genealogy from management theory brings with it the problematic imperative to acknowledge diversity, celebrate it, manage it, as if it were a human resource to be put to better use and, of course, greater profit. Indeed, the word circulates throughout US culture invoking an apparent concern for others, especially those less fortunate than ourselves, those located on the margins, those suffering still from systems of oppression—but for what purpose? What are we being interpellated into, asked to do, asked to become? I'd say not much. (453)

But as much as teachers and students alike are worn out by "diversity fatigue" (453), diversity *is* a performative, albeit an infelicitous one. The self-involved dialogue between Cain and Abel, pervasive claims to victimization, and an interest in guilt and shame: these cue diversity's performative nature. Then there are the material realities impacted by diversity's performance: college admissions, scholarship opportunities, the support offered by universities' multicultural offices. Public institutions—courts, legislative offices, and schools—structure understandings of race, and these structures have enacted, are based on, and potentially carry on America's vexing racial legacy. This is why it is so important that we reflect on Himley's question.

The task of seeing diversity discourse as an institutional performance of racial order has grown more unwieldy since the civil rights movements. As race theorists Michael Omi and Howard Winant have argued, the civil rights movement constituted a "great transformation": "Racial politics now take place under conditions of 'war of position,' in which minorities have achieved significant (though by no means equal) representation in the political system, and in an ideological climate in which the meaning of racial equality can be debated, but the desirability of some form of equality is assumed. The new 'rules of the game' thus contain both the legacy of movement efforts to rearticulate the meaning of race and to mobilize minorities politically on the basis of the new racial ideologies thus achieved, and the heritage of deep-seated racism and inequality" (88). Every time the battle dust of racial politics settles, it gets pitched afresh and further reconstituted by institutional shifts and altered cultural formations, whether these shifts in universities are sparked by "great books" debates, the neoconservative Students' Bill of Rights, or the current effort to push against persistent colorblind positions. The pervasive commitment to "diversity" in social institutions can be seen as an inheritance of these movements, even when refiguring earlier civil rights activism. Even as I agree with critiques of diversity, then, my goal is to revise rather than eradicate diversity discourse.

One challenge is that diversity calls up authentic bodies that are part of taken-for-granted racial categories. Race-conscious activists of the 1960s introduced a critical lens that exposed how social institutions had been and continued to be organized by race, and ever since, universities and other social institutions have explicitly adopted racial classification systems in order to further root out racial inequalities, for example, in student admissions, faculty hires, and curricula. But in recognizing the importance of racial difference, official diversity and multicultural discourses, in effect, have reified race and even implicitly naturalized racial difference (Gilyard "Higher Learning"; Hum). Paradoxically, even though racial categories are in the foreground, "race" as a historical concept and social construction has gone underground. The teacherly expectation of authentic voices acts out this misconception of race and thus interpellates racial minority students into ones who need to authentically perform their cultures. If racial minority students are positioned as those denied authentic voice, where does that leave unmarked white students?

Whiteness studies offers important reasons for identifying whiteness (Barnett; Nakayama and Krizek; Prendergast "Race") but also suggests reasons to be wary of essentialist constructions of "whiteness" that lock white students into guilt, shame, and anger (Keating; Winans). While shame may be a turning point in students' critical consciousness (Himley 458; Swiencicki), I share English studies scholar AnnLouise Keating's serious concern about pedagogies that invite guilt: "The point is not to encourage feelings of personal responsibility for the slavery, decimation of indigenous peoples, land theft, and so on that occurred in the past. It is, rather, to enable students of all colors more fully to comprehend how these oppressive systems that began in the historical past continue misshaping contemporary conditions. Guilt-tripping plays no role in this process. Indeed, guilt functions as a useless, debilitating state of consciousness that reinforces the boundaries between apparently separate 'races'" (915). Students are thus left to choose between injured and injuring subject positions. Because race is overdetermined, solutions tend to be off-point, irrelevant to countering systemic inheritances of a racist past. As compositionist Sue Hum tells us, "the cost of literacy for our students is to be *either* assimilated *or* to remain 'native-like'" (576).

To discuss race is precarious, a difficulty of preserving racial categories long enough to expose racial injustice while also teaching students to destabilize those categories that emerge from our nation's history of racism. Accordingly, this bind inspires a second set of counterproductive interpellations: individuals who claim race neutrality. Race neutrality may register resistance to the language of injury. Compositionist Amy E. Winans's insightful study suggests that race neutrality may be about "white safety," resulting from some white students' fear of re-performing racial injustice by recognizing racial difference. Whether or not fear of injuring—or fear of claims to injury—causes race neutrality, the effect is the same. Within our discipline's body of knowledge race operates as an "absent presence" (Prendergast "Race"), and within classroom discourse students manage to dodge race through a "rhetoric of evasion" (Leverenz). As a result of such discursive fumbling, race in university circles is typically understood through problematically reified categories or evaded entirely, and we thus face the unintended effects of multiculturalism: identity politics and divisive perceptions of campus diversity. In short, a rhetoric of injury can perpetuate the reification of racial categories, the dissipation of these categories into an "absent presence," and composition students' "diversity fatigue."

My argument is that the seemingly opposing tendencies either to overdetermine racial difference or to treat race as an absent presence evidence a rhetoric of injury, which presents students with difficulties that are helped but not necessarily resolved by fostering critical race consciousness among individuals. Donna LeCourt, in her introduction to *Identity Matters*, points to such limitations when she reflects on two students who developed a critical consciousness about identity and privilege but either chose to maintain or felt unable to change systems they deemed unfair. To be clear, my point is *not* to support those who would rather ignore racial injury, who would admonish that racial minorities need only to *get over it* and turn a colorblind eye to past and present injustice. Not at all. On the contrary, we need to develop a rigorous discourse that sheds light on the commonplace ways race works on campus. The problem with a rhetoric of injury is that, first, it seeks out exceptions, neither elucidating nor redressing the more subtle and commonplace inheritance of racism. Second, the only available subject positions are victims and aggressors. Third, the rhetoric of injury allows for counterproductive accusations of reverse discrimination that deny the present effects of past racism.

What we require is a careful revision of "injury" as the primary mediation of racial politics. Universities, in particular, have focused on injuries of exclusion, remedied by valuable inclusions of underrepresented students through admissions, minority faculty through hiring, and cultural histories through curricular reform. However, Gutiérrez-Jones cautions that an inclusion-exclusion paradigm forecloses other ways of thinking about racial accountability, that "racial inclusion as a remedy for discrimination (a particularly strong part of the 1980s 'cultural wars') has displaced questions of what happens after inclusion is achieved" (13). What happens after inclusion? What happens when, in composition pedagogy, "inclusion" typically means learning how to take on a particular discourse community's existing practices? What rhetorical tactics *could* we employ to foster cooperative and critical interracial relationships when race has become an absent presence? The following analysis of the Vietnamese American Coalition's participation in a democratic debate illustrates the ways students can be pulled into a rhetoric of injury and thus calls up the difficulties a rhetoric of injury produces even after inclusion is achieved.

VAC Students and a Liberal Logic of Inclusion

In 2002 VAC students were caught up in an interracial dispute not explicitly recognized as such. The issue: Was the undergraduate student body's funding of several student clubs' high school student mentorship programs constitutional, and by what process should the student government make this decision? When the conflict erupted in late May, I was a participant-observer studying the discourse practices of the VAC, which had been mentoring local Vietnamese and Vietnamese American high school students since 1995. In fact, most clubs that mentored high school students self-identified as "cross-cultural" organizations (read: racial minority) and moreover identified student government leaders as white, more specifically white "Greeks" (read: white fraternity and sorority members). So when VAC learned that the student government judicial board had made funding high school outreach programs unconstitutional—based on the liberal argument that student funding allocation should benefit all *individuals* in the undergraduate body equally (rather than affirm group rights)—discussions about constitutionality and democratic processes on campus grew tense.

Even when the cross-cultural student club leaders and the legislative representatives agreed, the existing democratic discourse frustrated their dialogue. Eventually the judicial board did revise the ruling to allow funding of student clubs' high school student mentorship programs but not until four years after the original ruling, when most of the students involved had graduated. More important, what those of us in universities require is deliberation about the student and wider campus discourses that structure understandings of racial difference. An account of VAC students' rhetorical response to the judicial board's decision reveals the problems created by a rhetoric of injury. By examining how VAC's chair, Bryan, made rhetorical preparations to argue for high school outreach funding and then educated a younger student into the campus democratic discourse, we see confirmation of the students' successful inclusion into the student government's democratic discourse, on the one hand, and why inclusion into the discourse community was inadequate, on the other.

The Vietnamese American Coalition's history suggests that the organization was a direct inheritance of 1960s Third World Liberation Front efforts toward inclusion, specifically the facilitation of racial minority students' admission into and participation in universities. These arguments for inclusion relied on a belief in liberal premises. As rhetorician Sharon Crowley explains, liberalism is a pervasive ideology in which its adherents believe in individual rights, equal opportunity, and freedom. "The liberal subject," according to Hugh Blair, is "that free and sovereign individual who can think his way through disagreements by resorting to reason and who authorizes the results of his investigation to his very ability to reason" (Crowley "Modern Rhetoric" 35). Presumably, after inclusion into the democracy—here, the democratic structure of the student body and its government—the liberal subject is then equal and free. To an extent, liberal belief in the "sovereign individual" has been a stepping-stone for early TWLF demands for "self-determination," or the right to determine one's own educational opportunities.

It was in this climate that VAC established a high school student mentorship program, in 1995, to facilitate Vietnamese American high school students' entry into university culture. Bryan, then a high school student, was in the first cohort of mentees. Seven years later, as an undergraduate senior and the current VAC chair, Bryan had firsthand knowledge of the possibilities of mentorship and found himself defending the program. On May 20, 2002, Bryan and peer student club leaders spent the day researching lines of argument to maintain funding for their high school outreach programs. Two weeks earlier, the student legislative representatives had informed them that the student government could no longer sponsor clubs' high school outreach programs with student body funds. The judicial board claimed that in 2001 they had received an anonymous letter challenging the constitutionality of allocating student body money to high school outreach programs.

Agreeing that such funding was unconstitutional, the judicial board wrote a letter to the legislative council and explained the decision on a public bulletin outside their office: "The [high school outreach] activities and programs are not open to the participation by the greater student body and thus do not benefit associated students. The critical argument that these programs benefit the facilitators is acknowledged, but the number of facilitators is not proportional to the budget allocation nor to the greater student body." Here, the emphasis on individualism seemed at odds with students' efforts to redress past racial injustice by mentoring racial minority youth into college life. As Crowley explains, "liberal pluralism harbors the hope that difference can be erased if only everyone will just be reasonable—which means something like 'think as we do'" ("Modern Rhetoric" 41). Indeed, "abstract liberalism" and an assumption of equal opportunity, according to critical race schol-ar Eduardo Bonilla-Silva's discussion of "color-blind racism," is often used as a framework to "ignore the effects of past and contemporary discrimination on the social, economic, and educational status of mi-norities" (31).

The legislative council soon charged a five-member judicial over-sight committee with the task of reviewing the judicial board's decision and would hold one more meeting before the oversight committee con-vened the next week. Dismayed that they had only learned of the judi-cial board's decision one year after the fact, the cross-cultural groups that sponsored high school outreach—which included cross-cultural clubs as well as the student government itself—wished to voice their concerns at the legislative council meeting. After a full day of research-ing arguments for high school outreach programs, Bryan's last task of the day was to rhetorically prepare younger student leaders at the VAC cabinet meeting; only Katie, VAC's freshman representative, and I, a participant-observer then mentoring two high school students, attend-ed that meeting on May 20.

The meeting became a teaching moment that demonstrates how these student leaders believed knowledge of appropriate rhetorical rea-soning would facilitate inclusion into the university community. Bryan opened by stating his purpose to "educate" us, especially Katie, who would need to learn about campus governance and politics. "We want to know just as much as them [the student government] if not more be-fore we start talking with anybody," he explained, walking us premise-by-premise through the judicial board's reasoning: because student gov-ernment "money comes straight from student fees," because "it's only right that what we pay we get back," and because high school outreach "is not directly benefiting this university's students," the judicial board decided that funding high school outreach was unconstitutional. Katie listened and offered possible counterarguments, which Bryan affirmed or revised according to his understanding of student government dis-course. For instance, he countered Katie's claims that VAC mentors are university students who benefit from the programs since this would not address the charge that benefits need to be proportionate to the entire student body.

Inclusion into the student government discourse seemed clear-cut. The hierarchy of student government, modeled after the national branches of government, and adherence to the constitution for legit-imate reasoning and to Robert's Rules of Order defined government officers' rhetorical practices. Without explicit knowledge of the consti-tution, Bryan knew, their assertions would seem irrelevant and mark their "outsiderness." As long as students played the right game, the liberal assumption was that individuals inherently held agency as university citizens and building coalitions of these voices would be an effective strategy. Through Bryan's leadership, VAC students allied themselves with pan-Asian Pacific American, Japanese American, Chicano/a, and African American student organizations. Bryan and his peer cross-cultural club leaders began to build a case challenging the fairness of the judicial board's decision-making process, their decision, and even the judicial oversight committee. They visited the cross-cultural center on campus to get information about the decision and the process by which it was made; they read the constitution and pored over the student body budget; they questioned whether the judicial board's reasons for ending high school outreach funding were consistent with other spending choices; they researched the makeup of the oversight committee, its function, and requirements to amend the constitution; and they spoke with other student leaders and university administrators to gain perspective.

Elaborating on their united rhetorical preparation, Bryan explained to Katie that these clubs would present the following arguments to the legislative council representatives: that the judicial board's decision-making process was unfair because the vice president was not given due notice (less than an hour to prepare for a preliminary hearing) to speak on behalf of the value of high school outreach programs to the student body; that the process excluded the testimony of all student clubs that participated in high school outreach programs; that the judicial board, in fact, did not directly notify these clubs of the challenge to funding or their ruling until one year after the decision; that the judicial oversight committee is self-interested as the constitution designates two judicial board officers to be on the oversight committee (essentially overseeing their own decision); that the constitution designates one staff member to be on the oversight committee when only students should vote on student government issues; and, finally, that the oversight committee's makeup lacks bylaws that would clarify the committee's self-interested nature.

If inclusion were indeed the only criteria for students' democratic participation, then these capable appeals based on democratic assumptions should have resolved the dispute. However, the discussion of the legislative council meeting tells a different story. The dominant democratic conventions were limited in two important ways. First, the democratic conventions mistakenly assumed that everyone's voice had equal weight when the playing field was not level; agency is not granted based on awareness of discourse conventions alone. Rather, because the fraternity system is among the oldest of university student organizations and because nonwhites had been historically segregated from educational institutions until relatively late in U.S. history, white students at this university had greater involvement in student governance. Rhetorical authority had arisen out of the social structures that authorized white students, specifically "Greeks," over racial minorities and the historically recent institution of "cross-cultural" student organizations. Second, because cross-cultural clubs were limited to responding to the judicial board's decision and to generating reasons validated by precedent, they could not confront issues of historical injustice against racial minorities and the present interracial tension. In particular, the students required a way to discuss race in the climate of a "majority minority" campus, where more than 40 percent of the student body that year identified as Asian or Asian American.

Although race did go underground in the legislative council meeting, that certainly did not mean race was absent from students' consciousness. In fact, racial identity politics most likely instigated the anonymous letter challenging that high school outreach programs (primarily for racial minorities) did not benefit the larger student body. Bryan made sure that Katie understood this: "All the big clubs, all the big cultural clubs are all saying this is wrong, you know. And we . . . talked to a lot of people, and one person in admin said, actually said, from what he hears, it sounds like somewhat of a racist, uh, prejudice against the cultural clubs and [the student government]." He emphasized his point by relaying a conversation he had with the student government president, who espoused the civil rights backlash characteristic of today's university culture:

> See, the president is also like . . . He told us one time . . . He said about our [high school outreach] conferences, "Well, they're somewhat exclusive, right?" Because we, we geared it toward minorities, right? People of color. He's all like . . . That's his argument. He's all, "Let's be realistic. Can I as a Caucasian male go to your conference, you know, and feel comfortable?" You know? I'm like, "You can go and do whatever you want to do. We don't exclude anybody. You can be part of our conference as long as you go to the training, da da da, do all the logistics."

The student president focused not on inclusion but exclusion, where white students were the victims. Despite Bryan's reading of campus racial politics, he withheld this perspective and chose to employ accepted lines of constitutional reasoning in the next day's more public forum. And he was not alone; no one mentioned the elephant in the room.

What Happens after Inclusion? (or When No One Mentions Race)

At the open legislative council meeting the next day, race went uninter-rogated and the result was not a productive democratic discussion. If the student democratic discourse was working, the legislative council meeting on May 21, 2002, should have been empowering: the legislative representatives agreed that the judicial board's decision was wrong-headed or at least the decision-making process was unfair, and they had invoked a judicial oversight committee; the representatives and student club constituents were dialoguing in an inclusive legislative council meeting; and the cross-cultural students were equipped with consti-tutional knowledge. All students involved in the discussion, student government representatives and cross-cultural organization leaders, were capable rhetors who relied on the ideal of a liberal democracy and whose active engagement in campus politics indicate best intentions to realize that ideal. But racial politics operated quietly and destructive-ly. The public forum of the legislative council meeting played out as a blame game—roving far from any situated historical understanding of racial injustice. This discussion interprets what happened after in-clusion, specifically in a climate of race-as-absent-presence, when VAC students used traditional democratic means for voicing their concerns in the university. In short, the rhetorical jostling by the legislative coun-cil and cross-cultural student organizations created shifting subject po-sitions and closed off discussion before it even began.

The next legislative council meeting, designated "open" and public, took place on May 21, 2002. Twenty-two legislative representatives sat on one side of the room, the head of the council with a gavel at the cen-ter and representatives with title plates on both sides of her, and more than thirty cross-cultural student club leaders and members filled in the other side of the room; racial identity politics was evident as almost all of the white students sat on one side and almost all of the nonwhite students sat on the other. VAC's chair Bryan, their freshman represen-tative Katie, one student member William, my high school mentee, and I attended the meeting on behalf of VAC. The moderator called the meeting to order, following Robert's Rules of Order's strict regulations of who could initiate speech or respond. When the moderator arrived at the agenda item on the judicial oversight committee, one cross-cultural club constituent raised the critique of the oversight committee's self-interested makeup. Although the council leader attempted to move on to the next agenda item, a murmur forced her back to the topic of the oversight committee and the judicial board's ruling on high school out-reach funding. With this halting start to the discussion, another cross

-cultural club member curtly asked whether the oversight committee meeting would be open to the public and received a vague answer that he should e-mail his legislative representative or judicial board members.

A few cross-cultural club representatives began to get agitated, and a few legislative representatives began to grow defensive. Cuing into this dynamic, a cross-cultural club constituent tried to bring them back together, saying: "I mean, I have a lot of respect for [the student government]. But with that comes a responsibility that you should have meetings open. I know it's not in the constitution [that the judicial oversight committee meeting be open or closed]. You represent us as constituents and us not having a voice. . . . We just want to talk about it, not attack one another. We just want to get our issues out." This student was responding to legislative representatives' shutting the cross-cultural students out of the discussion and also their positioning of cross-cultural clubs as "attack[ing]." Indeed, one or two of the thirty or so students' statements were delivered with vehemence, one interrupted a legislative representative mid-sentence; however, another student explained that the anger was not directed at the legislative representatives but it reflected their frustration at having no effective way of expressing their concerns to those students in power. After all, all of the students in the room supported the high school mentorship programs. Still, tensions mounted, and a division grew between the legislative council and the cross-cultural student groups.

Soon the students' discussion stumbled into a rhetoric of injury and the roles of injurer and injured slipped back and forth. As Gutiérrez-Jones has explained: "Injury is . . . a bit fickle as regards questions of agency. While one definition of the term emphasizes a willful action of hurt, and therefore a resulting blame, another definition treats injury as an effect without focus on the agent. In this sense, injury marks a dichotomy in legal thought that establishes distinct poles as adjudication works through either the perpetrator's or victim's perspectives. Extending the implications of this dichotomy, one might well argue that the competing basis for arguments about reverse discrimination and institutional racism are bound up in this slippage" (24). The legislative council meeting illustrates this slippage, where legislative representatives alternately positioned the racial minority students across from them as either those inflicting injury or as those injured. One legislative representative's statement encapsulates both sentiments at once: "You guys are, well, preaching to the wrong crowd. You're getting angry at us, and we're trying to help you out here. So I'm going to give you the best advice that I can right now, which is to take Cal for example and rally against it, against this decision. Hold a protest. Get students to support your actions, your claims, your arguments, your positions.

Go out there. Be seen by the student body. Most of the people who are out there on campus do *not* know what's going on." This representative presented the council as injured by the cross-cultural student clubs' anger ("You're getting angry at us") and proceeded to negate the council's power—ironic in light of the authority of their office. Rather, he advised that the students protest against the government of which he was a part, thus implying that they should take on the role of injured to achieve their goal. In referring to Berkeley protests, his statement alludes to civil rights and TWLF movements for inclusion and relies on the idea that everyone is equally authorized. This is why he could negate his own authority; he was just another individual. In historian Joan W. Scott's words: "Here we have not only an extreme form of individualizing, but a conception of individuals without agency" (17).

Even though several legislative representatives positioned the cross-cultural student clubs primarily as injurer and as using their anger to appeal emotionally and without textual backing, the club constituents were raising logical arguments. One student questioned the definition and procedures of the oversight committee; another commented on the lack of bylaws about the committee in the constitution; and still another called on the council's responsibility to represent them. While this rhetoric should have been acceptable, the head of the council still positioned the cross-cultural clubs as outside of the discourse community. She stated:

> Another clarification. The judicial board, it's not their job to represent [university] students. It's because they're appointed. It's their job to interpret the constitution. So if you guys want to talk to them about it or argue about them, you have to get the constitution and have constitutional background, your interpretation of the constitution. Because that is the only way that they will change their mind. Because if they see that there's constitutional backing as far as pulling high school outreach, then they won't reconsider. But as far as just talking to them and arguing with them about it, it's not gonna do anything because you're, you're going there, it's just kind of like, with blanks. You're not saying anything because you don't have any constitutional backing.

VAC chair Bryan retorted:

> First of all, I've read the constitution, okay? And there're supposed to be guidelines to this oversight committee, but there aren't. They're supposed to be in the bylaws, but I didn't see that in there, online.
>
> Second of all, there're supposed to be seven judiciary members, right? But I only counted five.

Third of all, 25 percent?! The last elections, we only had 22.7 percent total. To turn *out*. That's the best turn out we've had, so how are we supposed to get 25 percent to change the constitution?

Fourth of all, the rationale that they say that outreach does not represent [university] students [or] can ever help out any other people than ourselves? We can never go, let's say feed the homeless and use [student body] money to do so because those people are not [university] students. So if this comes down, so that's saying that our student groups can never help out the community, at least not with [student body] money, because that does not represent [university] students, right? That's their rationale. If that happens, as long as that occurs, that's just one thing we can never have the capacity to do.

Bryan and other members of cross-cultural clubs needed repeatedly to dodge the injurer-injured subject positions because these were inadequate to their proposed goals: to receive funding to mentor high school students. Bryan used logos to reposition himself as operating within democratic discourse conventions, and others refigured their ethos (e.g., "We just want to thank you for hearing our voices, for letting us bring our issues to the table" and "We are all in support of the same issues . . . we're your constituents").

Even when the cross-cultural student clubs refashioned the rhetoric of injury so that both they and their legislative representatives could hold more empowering positions, all students continued to fall back on a liberal logic of individualism. The student democracy worked under the assumption that individuals (regardless of race, class, gender) inherently have equal rhetorical agency, and in this system that assumes a level playing field, equality means treating everyone the same. That's why the judicial board's ruling assumes that the funding should benefit the student body proportionally. That's also why the legislative representatives kept returning the cross-cultural representatives to their own actions: students who objected to the judicial board's decision needed to help themselves. In suggesting that the cross-cultural student clubs voice their concerns to the board, to the staff director, to the larger student body, the legislative representatives believed in each student's rhetorical agency, believed in the weight of each student's voice.

Focusing exclusively on inclusion into a democratic system without interrogating the system itself can enable divisive racial politics and injustice to persist. The student president commended Bryan on noting that the bylaws failed to give guidelines for the oversight committee, and he admitted that the makeup of the oversight committee was flawed because its creation was an abuse of power by a former president who, fearing that he would be recalled, instituted a mechanism for his holding onto office. What's telling is not just the former president's abuse of power but also that he wasn't held in check; the president thus had the means to abuse the power of his office.

This is a point made repeatedly by critical race theorists: the system is unjust as a result of historical racial injustices that have left their traces on institutional structures—including the student government, student clubs, and university administration. Inclusion into an unjust system does not rectify the unjust system. The racial division between representatives and their constituents was not surprising, especially in light of Bryan and his peer cross-cultural leaders' belief that the student government was dominated by white fraternities and sororities. Legislative and judicial officers did not just have authority by virtue of their office; their office was a benefit garnered from unacknowledged white privilege. One way to expose the absent presence of race and thereby expose the unjust system is through a critical historical engagement in which we identify the social structures that allow the racial injustice to persist. The students needed an interpretive framework that would enable them to analyze how their institutional structures—government offices, student organizations, and general democracy—were inflected by a history of race.

SEARCHING FOR A "CRITICAL RACE PRAXIS"

Within the university, college writing faculty are in a position to foster students' rhetorical engagement within their campus communities; such work could encourage students to critically read a rhetorical context that matters to them and to articulate their concerns accordingly. We can begin by interrogating the knotted racial politics on our campuses. A rhetoric of injury (and what Gutiérrez-Jones has called the "logic of moral equivalence") may help adjudicate acts of blatant racism but is ill-suited to the more subtle ways social structures carry on racial legacies without participants' intentions. The students at the meeting were after all on the same side, and they were in positions of authority. Critical race theorist Eric K. Yamamoto has challenged that race discourse often tends to focus on "acts of invidious discrimination" like housing discrimination or "horrific acts of domination" like ethnic cleansing. In our classes we might invent with our students a "critical race praxis" that addresses the more subtle and even unintended ways racial legacies continue to impinge on speakers and writers today—a praxis that helps us understand the "oftentimes mundane deployment of subordinating social, economic, and political structures" (Yamamoto 84–85). As a start, composition pedagogy must challenge a pervasive belief in the logic of individualism, the belief that inclusion and awareness of academic rhetorical conventions alone will eradicate unequal rhetorical agency. A critical race praxis, I propose, requires a deep sociohistorical inquiry into articulations of race over time as well as serious deliberation over community values.

An interrogation into the history of racialization enables students to explore how speaking positions are differentially authorized and to question how historically unequal access to mainstream universities shaped their system of student government representation, fraternities and sororities, and minority student organizations and coalitions. As Scott argues in her essay on multiculturalism's shortcomings, a more productive discourse about race would focus on "enunciations" of difference: "It makes more sense to teach our students and tell ourselves that identities are historically conferred, that this conferral is ambiguous (though it works precisely and necessarily by imposing a false clarity), that subjects are produced through multiple identifications, some of which become politically salient for a time in certain contexts, and that *the project of history is not to reify identity but to understand its production as an ongoing process of differentiation*, relentless in its repetition, but also and this seems to me the important political point— subject to redefinition, resistance, and change" (19, emphasis mine). College writing courses can help students step away from us-them and you-me identity politics by encouraging students to do such historical work. Histories of mainstream American universities clearly tell us that enrollment at early mainstream universities in the United States was reserved for white male students and that these early generations of students created valuable student organizations of debate clubs, literary societies, and fraternities. But because nonwhite students were historically excluded from mainstream universities and because fraternities are among the oldest student organizations, the Greek fraternity system built a tradition of leadership that places white students more firmly within university student governance.

As I learned about VAC students' concerns, I began to see that these students and their peers already had working knowledge of the ways racial difference was historically enunciated in mainstream universities, and their understanding of the rhetorical situation illustrates historical work that we might adapt to the classroom. Bryan commented on differentiated student authority:

> So, we thought at least [the student government] would support us. But no, they're not. And see, they tell us, "Well, you should send a representative. Someone should run for something." We *have*. We, we've run for things, but the thing is the people—90 percent of the people that are elected or win elections have a, have a background in Greek organizations. Meaning they get their fellow Greeks to vote for them. And Greeks have a lot of power on this

campus. Asian Greeks are separate from Greeks. We don't have voting, like we don't have a Greek council. Asian Greeks are on their own.

Bryan was not alone in his perception. The next year, in a letter to the college newspaper, an undergraduate was cynical about the "Greek" dominance in student government and that group's ability to determine the student body's social and political direction; she argued that fraternities and sororities do not represent the student body's concerns. With their long history, fraternities have effectively institutionalized themselves within and networked beyond universities. Bryan argued that the authority of this student organization has been limited to white fraternities and sororities. Quite simply, race-conscious student organizations—whether political, social, or disciplinary—have a more recent history because significant numbers of nonwhites have only entered U.S. universities relatively recently in the nation's history.

To complicate matters, race has been rearticulated in major ways since the civil rights movement and related Third World Liberation Front strikes, and several VAC students had learned about this history in Asian American and other ethnic studies courses. The undergraduate curriculum reflects multiple ethnic studies traditions, students create and participate in "cross-cultural" organizations, and university administrators fund programs to promote diversity and community outreach. This university, specifically, is not only a majority-minority campus but also an Asian/Pacific Islander American majority campus. The university's office of institutional research reports that in the fall of 2002, 44.5 percent of the student body was Asian/Pacific Islander, 26.1 percent White/Caucasian, 2.1 percent African American/Black, 10.4 percent Chicano/Latino, and 0.4 percent Native American. The response has been backlash. In the fall quarter after the high school outreach funding dispute, a student wrote a satirical opinion in the student newspaper that aptly indexed uneasy racial politics. "I propose to create a new community within the university that has long been overdue," the student began. "There is a vacancy in the herd of our campus's multicultural atmosphere and I aim to fill it." Then: "I present the Caucasian American Coalition." Even if his introduction is facetious, the proposal points to the university's complex interracial climate. Since university cultural and material resources are limited, we might identify in the article's argument ("Don't forget us! We need Caucasian American Studies too") a larger tension that is about rhetorical positioning, cultural and material resources, and democracy.

When naming racial categories and using these categories to structure curricula, academic programs, student organizations, and funding opportunities, universities not only respond to historical racial injustices but they also revise complex exigencies for students, which impact their ability to rhetorically compete for resources. In her research on Asian American activism, Asian American studies scholar Linda Trinh Võ has stated that "state bureaucracies, unwilling to deal with the intricacies of subgroup difference, initiate new aggregate racial categories that can inadvertently activate group mobilization. . . . These classification systems, once institutionalized, become the basis for the distribution of resources by presenting groups with a particular logic for collective action" (6). The editorial writer understood these campus interracial politics but only in *ahistorical* terms. For this reason he could draw on commonplaces in multiculturalism's presentist discourse (e.g., claims of "underrepresent[ation]," a desire to "celebrate" white American culture), employing these rhetorical devices to argue for resources and agency within the current university economy. But he misunderstands that more recent articulations of race do not make earlier articulations simply disappear; rather, the concept of race now bears its cumulative rearticulations.

It was only from an ahistorical perspective that this white male student could position white males as victims, injured from an alleged absence from university studies. In actuality, an examination of existing student organizations showed that his anxiety over race-conscious student organizations dominating the student body was not justified. The university student affairs office described the organizations on campus, indicating that there are fifty-two fraternities and sororities compared to only twenty-nine "cross-cultural" student organizations. Student academic clubs outnumber both. Another student newspaper article suggested that many students recognized the tension among student organizations and the dominance of Greeks in student government, and as a result, the students organized a leadership forum to deliberate on their mutual concerns.

In composition pedagogy we might take a cue from the VAC students and their peers, who were acculturated into and at times actively sought historical understanding of their university communities. Composition teachers often do a good job of asking students to research audience perspectives and to research their perspectives as writers. We might, moreover, ask students to inquire into the ways subject positions are historically conferred and thereby interpellate them as writers and readers. In this case study the student government officers and the cross-cultural student club leaders could arrive at a more textured sense of race by reconsidering racial differentiation historically and, through this lens, reexamine the possibilities and limitations of mentoring students into their university community. This undertaking requires sophisticated interpretation and composition abilities that can accommodate the multiple and ambiguous meanings of race, investigate how such meanings may still be sedimented in their social structures, and identify the effects of this continued racialization on their present circumstances. These students had already started the hard work of interpreting the subject positions available to them—peeling back the layers of histories of American universities, of racial minority students' activism in the 1960s, and of the growth of the extracurriculum. But examining the sociohistorical construction of subject positions is only a start. Beyond fostering students' understandings of the rhetorical landscape generated by racial differentiation, the rhetorical education in composition classrooms could continue with inquiry into what students will do with newfound understandings of their campuses. That is, if we are to generate a critical race praxis in our classrooms, our discussions should involve careful deliberation over community values that will direct future action.

A rhetoric informed by the commonplace of social responsibility—one in which students productively recognize and make use of their authority, rather than personal injury, in which students deny *all* agency—would better enable students to forward their democratic rhetoric. What would be possible if students were to historicize the institutions that differentially authorized their speaking positions? What would be possible if students examined the ways a contemporary structuring of race—for example, the ubiquitous university valuing of diversity—impacted their rhetorical exigencies? And what would happen if students deliberated community values with these more textured understandings of race? In chapters 4 and 5, I consider the rhetorical practices that VAC students used to both recognize their ethnic and racial pasts and to re-perform the subject positions available to Vietnamese American and, more generally, to American speakers and writers.

Chapter 4

Asian American Rhetorical Memory, a "Memory That Is Only Sometimes Our Own"

We have a memory of water. Ankle deep, back bent by the sun, verdant fields. Shallow basins, eyes sealed with tears, ornate cathedrals. Salt water shrouds, lips cracked, silent flotillas. We have a memory of water. A memory that is only sometimes our own.

—Barbara Tran, Monique T. D. Truong, and Luu Truong Khoi, eds.,
Watermark: Vietnamese American Poetry and Prose

Memory (the deliberate act of remembering) is a form of willed creation. It is not an effort to find out the way it really was—that is research. The point is to dwell on the way it appeared and why it appeared that way.

—Toni Morrison, "Memory, Creation, and Writing"

The willful desire to claim a "memory that is only sometimes our own," the unremitting imperative to rearticulate cultural memory, is fundamental to Asian American rhetoric. In early March 2000 a struggle over memory—who remembers, what gets remembered, and to what effect—pressed Asian American activists to protest against Senator John McCain's reference to "gooks." While campaigning for the Republican presidential nomination, McCain recalled his years as a Vietnam War prisoner-of-war and referred to North Vietnamese soldiers as "gooks." Criticism of his use of a racial slur ensued, and the news media who followed McCain's Straight Talk Express bus gave the story brief treatment. Was McCain repentant? No, he was entitled to his memory and speech. The *New York Times* quoted him on February 18: "I will continue to refer to them in language that might offend some people here, because of their beating and killing and torture of my friends. I hated the gooks and I will hate them for as long as I live." A few more days passed before he apologized, but the apology felt delayed, even reluctant. When the Straight Talk Express bus rolled into Southern California's Little Saigon in March, an Asian American student activist organized a protest to counter McCain's racialization of the Vietnamese prison guards. What was at stake was a contest over cultural memory—a struggle between McCain's understanding of "gook" as a personal memory (and perhaps also a nationalist one), on the one hand, and the activists' recall of the word from cultural memories that have effectively racialized Asians and Asian Americans, on the other.

The Asian American need to *re*member the American imaginary with Asian American peoples is poetically declared by the Vietnamese American editors of *Watermark*: "We have a memory of water" (Tran, Truong, and Khoi 224). If we understand that the Vietnamese word for "water" (*nước*) also means "nation," the declaration becomes a claim to not only a Vietnamese American memory but also a national memory. Quite simply, memory is central to Asian American rhetoric—a rejoinder to the persistent forgetfulness that displaces Asian Americans from commonplace understandings of what is American and also an opening up that fosters the "willed creation" of Asian American solidarity. Asian American rhetorical memory, then, has most often articulated *counter*memories that destabilize and then constitute anew the American subject. And yet, even though it is clear that activist racial projects since the yellow power movement of the 1960s and 1970s have been about recovering and claiming entitlement to cultural memories, important questions remain: What is the nature of a *rhetorical* memory in Asian American cultural production? What recollecting practices could Asian American speakers and writers use to shake up an objective notion of cultural memory and also appreciate the lived realities that make up Asian American history?

This chapter throws light on the ways the protest and, more important, the protest organizer Duc's later recollection of the conflict register larger concerns surrounding rhetorical memory: the conditions that call up Asian American rhetoric, the struggles over entitlement to memory, and the strategic and layered recall of past Asian American experiences. Duc, then a local university student who belonged to the Vietnamese American Coalition, told me about the protests in an interview. As he wove together the "gook" utterance amid multiple cultural memories, the fabric of his memory work became important to making meaning of the utterance. Notably, what makes Duc's performance of rhetorical memory possible is earlier advocacy for Asian Americans' right to participate in cultural memory work.

What follows is a discussion of the renewed interest in memory within Asian American studies and rhetorical studies since the 1960s. Drawing on this rhetorical heritage, I examine Duc's rhetoric as a performance of long-embattled claims to memory that have been building momentum over the past half-century. His account of the conflict gives us a glimpse into the ways rhetorical memory shifts in relation to changing racial constructions of Asian Americans. These shifts are not simply about archaeological shifts to different memorial *objects* but, more so, the epistemological shifts that guide the *practice* of how to remember and how to articulate memories. In this post–civil rights movement conflict, as Duc's recall so aptly illustrates, Asian American memory production involves threading together plural memories among plural loci and cultivating a related appreciation for *copia*. To be sure, such rhetorical production of Asian American memory is instructive to our understanding of memory as rhetorical art and social engagement.

RENEWED INTEREST IN THE RHETORICAL ART OF MEMORY

Memory is surely no stranger to rhetorical or related cultural studies. In fact, with the oft-cited "social turn" of the 1960s, memory saw renewed interest from rhetorical studies, ethnic studies, literary theory, philosophy, anthropology, history, and sociology. The inquiry has grown, in part, as a result of concerted efforts to lend value to marginalized voices and to complicate dominant histories: What memories have been suppressed? Which memories are legitimated and why? For the Asian American movement in the 1960s and 1970s, the conscious remembering of past Asian American realities played a large part in that historical moment's activism, and it is on the shoulders of these activist scholars that Asian Americans like Duc and I stand.

As important as the movement's memory work has been to our understanding of Asian American racial formation, these early approaches to memory problematically tended less toward the rhetorical and more toward what rhetorician Sharon Crowley has described as "methodical memory," or the modern preference for objective representation (*Methodical Memory*). Such methodical memory ironically risked reifying racial categories while critiquing that same racialization. Still, these and related energetic efforts to "dwell" are important as they have resulted in fruitful inquiry into the practice of *rhetorical* memory in the decades since the 1960s.

Early Activism for Asian American Engagement in Cultural Memory

Not surprisingly, calls for cultural memory were prominent in the Asian American movement, which was more broadly about claiming a politicized Asian American identity that challenged the juridical, pseudoscientific, and cultural racialization of Asian American bodies—named Mongol, Oriental, Asiatic, and yellow peril—reiterated in the United

States at least since the nineteenth century. The 1960s appropriation of the race-based identity "Asian American" marked an unprecedented coalition whose formation, in turn, led to a political rhetoric. For the movement's activists, the purpose of recollection was to attend to past Asian American realities as well as to challenge the persistent forgetting of the historical processes that have made Asian Americans a racial other. After all, as compositionists Jacqueline Jones Royster and Jean C. Williams have argued in "History in the Spaces Left," exclusionary histories distort our "interpretive frameworks" (564): Asian Americans continue to be read as the "foreigner-within" (Lowe); our contributions to America made inconsequential; and racial injustices obscured by constructions of Asian Americans as race-neutral ethnics (Omi and Winant).

Early in the movement, Asian American memory work was about challenging distorted representations of history and recovering Asian American experiences. *Roots: An Asian American Reader*, published through UCLA in 1971, was one early effort at this kind of recovery (Tachiki, Wong, and Odo). A collection of sociological and historical academic essays as well as "contemporary expression of the Asian American condition by the people themselves," *Roots* was meant to be read as "a documentary of our time" (vii). Editor Franklin Odo wrote that *Roots* signified the dual purpose of "going to the 'roots' of the issues facing Asians in America" and discussing how "our 'roots' go deep into the history of the United States . . . [to] explain who and what we are and how we became this way" (vii–viii). He continued: "Disregarding or misinterpreting the background of the particular group is one of the most important reasons for the failure to make meaningful changes in the ethnic community" (ix). The emphasis on uncovering "roots," recording a "documentary collection," and making accurate interpretations suggests that the editors would tell the *real* story. Similarly, over a decade later, Elaine H. Kim's *Asian American Literature: An Introduction to the Writings and Their Social Context*, published in 1982, was another first—the first book-length entry into Asian American literary scholarship—that was to remove distortions from cultural memory. Asian American literature, she explained, must be understood within "sociohistorical and cultural contexts . . . because, when these contexts are unfamiliar, the literature is likely to be misunderstood and unappreciated" (Kim xv). Such statements presuppose that there is a true understanding and appreciation of Asian American literature.

Memory in *Roots* and *Asian American Literature* was to serve as a corrective to the prevailing dismissal of Asian American culture, but in this way both Odo and Kim risked adopting not a rhetorical but a modern understanding of memory. The problem with a modern social realism approach to Asian American culture is that such approaches may reify an authentic and unchanging Asian American identity and history and thus trouble the writers' critique of existing overdetermined constructions of Asian Americans. Sharon Crowley's *The Methodical Memory: Invention in Current-Traditional Rhetoric* is instructive to understanding the prevalence of modern memory. She explains that only in relatively recent history has memory become arhetorical, an objective representation of past reality. During modernism, rhetorical practices were heavily influenced by efforts to advance scientific inquiry and reason, and memory assumed a positivist epistemology. Memorizing began with sensory perception, recall entailed accurate investigations of reality, and language would accurately translate the memory.

Perhaps because *Roots* and *Asian American Literature* were firsts, an appeal to modern representation could be attributed to the need to strategically legitimize such perspectives within academe, especially when Asian American studies was in its infancy. Or perhaps such texts only appeared to offer true representations because there were few to no related texts against which one might destabilize the category of Asian American. Regardless, these early subversions of cultural memory offered a crucial springboard for the growth of an Asian American *rhetorical* memory that would seek not simply to uncover but to articulate cultural memories and to interpret the ways such articulations mediate our understandings of memories.

Rhetorical Memory and an Appreciation for *Copia*

As many scholars across disciplines have engaged in memory, it has become clearer that the concept of memory as a rhetorical art requires deeper understanding. Indeed, memory studies has emerged as a result of fundamental questions raised by historian Pierre Nora about the relationship between history and memory and by Judaic studies scholar James Young about memory, trauma, and representation. Compositionist Marion Joan Francoz argues that memory studies must respond to postmodern skepticism against reified memory that functions as cultural indoctrination. In modern and postmodern epistemologies, we find the reasons for memory's curious absence from contemporary rhetorical theory. These epistemologies result in memory's double erasure, once by modern epistemology that relegates memory to individual mimetic representation and again by extreme forms of postmodernism that fear cultural indoctrination and its memorial conduit. Attributing the decline of *rhetorical* memory to a postmodern suspicion of memory, she supports challenges against modernist cultural reproduction but also questions extreme forms of postmodernism and their "fear of cultural enslavement" (26). What the postmodern questioning of dominant modern memory does offer us, however, is the understanding that memory is subjective and always partial. A critical approach to memory, she proposes, depends on diversity and "strong competing voices" (25).

Still, memory, according to anthropologists Jacob J. Climo and Maria G. Catell, is marked by "imprecision of concept" and "lack of theoretical development" (5). Rhetoricians John Frederick Reynolds and Kathleen Welch have each contended that the art of memory requires clarification in terms of its form, production, interpretation, and social life (Reynolds; Welch). Long before the modern emphasis on scientific inquiry, classical rhetoricians had heralded memory as the custodian of all the canons of rhetoric. By juxtaposing the unlikely pairing of classical and medieval rhetoric, on the one hand, and Sucheng Chan's 1991 *Asian Americans: An Interpretive History* and David Palumbo-Liu's 1999 *Asian/American: Historical Crossings of a Racial Frontier*, on the other, I suggest that we might arrive at a working understanding of rhetorical memory in general and Asian American rhetorical memory in particular.

While most students of the Western rhetorical tradition call to mind ancient mnemonic exercises when considering memory, it is important to understand that the art of memory was selective, crafted, and textured (Carruthers; Havelock; Reynolds; Yates). Mary Carruthers's *The Book of Memory*, a study of medieval monastic memory and its classical rhetorical heritage, offers an impressive theoretical articulation of memory's social life. To begin, the practice of gathering memories started with introspective investigation, which theologian Albertus Magnus called "the 'tracking down' (*investigatio*) of what has been 'set aside' (*obliti*) through and by means of memory" (Carruthers 20). Such recollection calls up not the real-world referent but the memorial symbols, thus relying on a complex system of signification. "Because it recalls signs," Carruthers writes, "reminiscence is an act of interpretation, inference, investigation, and reconstruction, an act like reading" (25). And an act like writing.

But this only began the process that made memory public. Gathering memories was a composition process, refined through copia and suitability to the occasion. Copia, in particular, was the measure of good memory, referring to the abundant layering of memories. The point was not, as in modernism, to retrieve a single accurate memory. Rather, copious recollection meant weaving together memories to produce a plural and textured composition. Finally, "public memory," elaborates Carruthers, "is a needed ethical resource for its contents complete the edifice of each individual's memory" (185). Just as the public would complete the individual, individuals had the civic and moral responsibility to share their memorial compositions in public realms. This meant that, in composing, rhetors should tailor memorial compositions for their intended audience and speaking occasion. The social nature of memory was basic to medieval rhetoric, for "an author who does not share his work and launch it, as it were, into the stream of literature is thought to be guilty of a sin against community" (208). Memory, then, was essential to the creating and sustaining of cultural heritage and community identity. The art of memory was traditionally about thoughtfully investigating memorial signs, interweaving memories, and thereby engaging the public to which one belonged.

For scholars like Sucheng Chan and David Palumbo-Liu, Asian American recollection has proceeded with an investigation of memorial traces across not only mental loci but the cultural sites tied up with Asian American history. The term "cultural memory," for rhetorician Winifred Horner, refers to the institutions that house memory (e.g., libraries, schools, popular media, etc.) (Reynolds 11). But given our histories, Asian American scholars have grown increasingly interested in the national and transnational sites that become sites of cultural memory. Chan's *Asian Americans*, for instance, illustrates the ways Asian American rhetorical memory is mapped onto the cultural sites of migration. Rather than begin the Asian American history with the commonplace of immigration experiences in the United States, she recenters the history on the emigration-immigration hyphen and cautions that her narrative is "an interim effort" and "interpretive"; the history thereby creates an opening for additional memorial work.

Palumbo-Liu's *Asian/American* more emphatically focuses on memorial practices that migrate among national and transnational cultural sites. He writes: "The role of memory becomes increasingly significant, as individuals and groups trace their relation to place, even as those traces may be covered over or erased, overlaid with different memories or claims to possession, as well as with memories and histories from different lands that have been brought over as part of the psychic makeup of dispossessed peoples and which constitute an irredactable perceptual grid through which the diasporic landscape is read" (218). The attention to multiple places with historical layers invigorates the production of *plural* memories, and this "irredactable" performance of copia dispels the authority of any single memory. In fact, Palumbo-Liu suggests that it is this preference for copia that makes architect Maya Lin's design of the Vietnam War Memorial so powerful; that is, "the abstract memorial rejects the literalizing and therefore stabilizing and codifying function of the realistic memorial" (252).

Together, the memorial work practiced by these Asian American scholars indicates a shared interest in rememorializing Asian American racial formation in the United States and, at the same time, a glimpse of the complexity of memory work. The memorial imperative among "yellow power" activists led to authentic representations of Asian American experience that could offset a naturalized conception of Asian Americans as foreigners. But as Toni Morrison has emphasized, memory is a "deliberate act"—not only recovery but also production, copious production. For Asian Americans, whose histories are formed through the transnational ties among Asia and the United States, an investigation into memory entails journeying through the cultural sites of memory (whether those sites are institutions, specific locales, or nations) and knitting together these memorial traces; this memory work weaves together Asian American heritage. Moreover, Asian American rhetorical memory, the copious (even if contradictory) investigation across cultural sites, demands tailoring to particular social conditions and moments. It is this rhetorical art that we see among the Asian American activists in the "American Gook" protest.

RECOLLECTING "GOOK" THROUGH ASIAN AMERICAN MEMORIES

Recollecting "gook" critically requires an investigation into how past uses of the sign could impact its present (and future) meaning, and the Asian American activist leading the protest was armed with both an Asian American studies background and rhetorical agility. Duc was an undergraduate student at a Southern California university, when in early 2000 newspapers were reporting that Senator John McCain, a contender for the Republican presidential nomination and a former Vietnam War POW, was initially unapologetic about calling former North Vietnamese prison guards "gooks" (Nevius). An apology did in fact come. *Washington Post* writer Rajiv Chandrasekaran reported on February 28: "'I will continue to condemn those who unfairly mistreated us,' McCain said. 'But out of respect to a great number of people whom I hold in very high regard, I will no longer use the term that has created such discomfort. I deeply regret any pain I have caused. . . . I apologize and renounce all language that is bigoted and offensive.'" The apology and the protests that followed embody competing readings of the cultural memories surrounding "gook," evident in the sharp disparity between McCain's representational memory and Duc's rhetorical memory.

No doubt, McCain's reliance on a modern representational understanding of memory directly contrasted with Duc's stated belief in the creative capacity of memory and the ways memories require critical interpretation. McCain composed memories to represent his experiences, calling up memories of war (recalling abuses), camaraderie (remembering his military friends), and new alliances (listening to the memories of South Vietnamese POWs). By recollecting his military service in the war and objecting to the abuses he endured, McCain effectively created alliances with U.S. veterans as well as many anticommunist Vietnamese Americans who shared his disdain for the North Vietnamese military. To a large extent, his rhetoric worked in that his controversial statements were treated briefly. In fact, an article in the *San Francisco Chronicle*, one day after the protest, proclaimed: "Little Saigon Opens Arms for McCain; Vietnamese Americans Dismiss His Use of Slur" (Marinucci). The article noted that the senator was "flanked onstage by nearly a dozen former Vietnamese soldiers who also were POWs."

It is worth noting, however, that while McCain's statements were rhetorical in terms of speaking to the cultural expectations of his audience, his treatment of *memory* was positivist. The apology and his "straight talk" mantra indicate a modern representational conception of language. That is, McCain adopted a modern epistemology, one that thwarted the possibility of understanding the rhetorical construction and impact of his utterance. With his brand of "straight talk," he suggested that "gook" was an objective signifier that referred only to specific prison guards who imprisoned him for five and a half years, not all Asians. He could maintain his "hate" because his apology suggested that the problem was his audience's "discomfort." Rather, I would argue that the problem went beyond the immediate exchange between speaker and audience; the problem is that each iteration of a racial epithet continues to reproduce a culture in which racializing is the norm. McCain, however, believed that the word applied only to the intended referent (specific prison guards) and to his personal memories, but for Asian American activists the use of "gook" was tangled up in a cultural memory of American racial violence. Neither McCain's apology nor his recollection of military service acknowledged the legacy of racism and racial violence cued by the word. Asian American activists were jarred by McCain's insistent use of a racial slur, so when the senator's campaign visited Southern California's Little Saigon (the country's largest Vietnamese American community), Duc had marked "American Gook" on T-shirts and organized a protest rally.

In contrast to McCain, who characterized "gook" in purely modern representational language that recalled his war trauma, Duc recalled the word's copious meanings. Duc fervently recounted his memory of the "American Gook" protest in an interview for me two years later, in 2002; this interview was part of my ethnographic case study of the political student organization the Vietnamese American Coalition (VAC). By then, Duc was a fourth-year undergraduate who had been active in the student organization for several years. As a poet, a political science major, and an Asian American student activist, he understood that to remember is to create. Asian American rhetorical memory played into the copious ways he traced past uses of "gook."

Duc began his account by recalling how he, then a student leader in VAC, had difficulty persuading other officers to challenge McCain. In this telling, he placed the word "gook" among multiple memorial traces ranging from McCain's utterance to hate crimes that took place in 1982 and 1996, from the Vietnam War to California's largest Little Saigon community.

> Duc: I went up to the cabinet members, and I said, "Oh, please be out here, you know, we need the numbers." And cabinet members, mostly guys, said, "We have an intramural basketball game that night." So, they can't be out there, right? Because they're playing an intramural basketball game.
>
> HH: How did you describe this issue to them? Or did they already know?
>
> Duc: They pretty much knew. And if they didn't, I told them that, you know, it's, it's wrong. We can't allow a public figure, any public figures, anybody that has influence upon people to use that kind of language, to use the term so casually. *And* to convince our community that "gook" equals "communist"? Because it does not. And how Vincent Chin was killed because of racial slurs and anti-people-of-color sentiment. Thien Minh Ly, you know our own Vietnamese American brother who was killed. And how racial slurs dehumanize people and lead to hate crimes.
>
> If VAC claims to be a political organization and represent the community, we *have* to be out there.

The word "gook," like most words, has many memorial traces that index past uses and varied signification. But what makes Duc's discourse an instance of rhetorical memory is his persuasive stitching together of a series of seemingly disparate moments and cultural sites. Each recalled moment or site contributes to a memorial composition whose sum is greater than all its parts and whose effectiveness becomes a catalyst for the group's response to McCain.

To begin, Duc called up McCain's "gook" utterance to reread its rhetorical impact. What McCain overlooked was what the Asian American protesters knew too well: memory confers significance on signs, especially charged ones like "gook." By identifying McCain as a "public figure," Duc not only commented on the reach and authority of McCain's speech but also read the public figure as embodying the state, itself a site of cultural memory. McCain's representational approach to language results in a "memory that is only sometimes our own," and in this way the state is a site that contains struggle over cultural memories.

Duc then presented a series of fragments ("*and* to . . ."; "and how . . ."; "and how . . .") that place the meaning of "gook" in other sites and thus destabilized McCain's statement that "gook" referred only to the North Vietnamese soldiers who kept him imprisoned.

Turning from a focus on a McCain-centered memory of war, the fragment that follows foregrounds the Vietnam War but shifts the emphasis from military conflict to the present-day Little Saigon community: "*And* to convince our community that 'gook' equals 'communist'?" For many in the diasporic community, "communist" signaled not simply the soldiers who imprisoned McCain but a phantom object of resentment in Little Saigon. The result was that McCain had many supporters in Little Saigon who did not know about, who forgave, or who condoned his use of "gook" to describe the North Vietnamese. Veterans of the South Vietnamese military literally stood beside him onstage during the political rally. In fact, some attendees cathected so strongly with McCain, they spat on and yelled "communist" at Duc and his fellow protesters. But by centering the Vietnamese American community within this war reference, Duc recentered "gook" within the cultural memory of the Vietnamese American immigrant and American-born community, and he argued that this local ethnic community needed to reject such racializing language. This memorial trace begins to unseat the primacy of McCain's memories without necessarily disregarding his experiences.

Threading together these traces of "gook" into the memories of McCain's rhetoric and the diasporic community, Duc's memorial investigation turned to two other uses of racial epithets against Asian Americans, hate crimes where racial epithets aggravated and even encouraged interracial violence: the murders of Vincent Chin in 1982 and Thien Minh Ly in 1996. Vincent Chin was a victim of hate crime, memorialized in the 1988 documentary *Who Killed Vincent Chin?* In 1982, in the midst of anti-Japanese attitudes resulting from Michigan's depressed auto industry, a white employee from Chrysler and his son beat a Chinese American man to death with a baseball bat. The documentary introduces the conflict as beginning with the murderers' comments about Chin's race, which they erroneously assumed was Japanese. The more recent case of Vietnamese American Thien Minh Ly, in 1996, was also a hate crime framed by racial epithets. Gunner Lindberg and his friend beat, stomped, and stabbed Ly, a twenty-four-year-old who was rollerblading near a community tennis court in California. Journalist Greg Hernandez's "Grisly Account of Ly Killing Believed Penned by Suspect" in the March 7, 1996, issue of the *Los Angeles Times* said that Lindberg wrote in a letter to a friend in prison, "Oh, I killed a jap a while ago" and detailed how he had killed Ly. Hernandez continues: "In a four-page letter filled with casual mentions of birthday plans, a friend's new baby, and the need for new tattoos, Gunner J. Lindberg may have also laid out a murder confession that led police directly to his door in their search for the killer of the 24-year-old Ly."

Duc layered these racially motivated crimes in his recall of McCain's "gook" statements and thereby foregrounded the ways language racializes. These threads point to the violent anger directed against Asians and Asian Americans, as in Chin's case, and the casual dehumanizing of Asians and Asian Americans, as in Ly's case. The threads of these memories weave back into McCain's own anger against the North Vietnamese "gooks" and his own casual use of the racial slur. Those who have seen the documentary *Who Killed Vincent Chin?* know that the atrocities of Chin's murder resulted in a national Asian American movement, indicating the racism was a national phenomenon and not the aberration of two men. The trial against Chin's murderers resulted in a three-year probation and a three-thousand-dollar fine. The ease with which two men could beat to death a Chinese American sparked a national controversy, eventually leading to a civil rights case against the men, but both were exonerated. By alluding to this famous case, Duc invoked the Asian American activism that grew out of the trial and activists' efforts to organize against injustice.

The fabric of Duc's recollection knits together traces of a public figure's rhetoric about war trauma, the Little Saigon community's ambivalence over Vietnamese communists, and the place of "gook" within cultural memories of hate crime—all of which seamlessly lead to Duc's final critique: "how racial slurs dehumanize people and lead to hate crimes." The composition therefore calls up a troubling association between racial slurs and hate-driven racial violence, an association that recasts McCain's war trauma in terms of the dehumanizing effects of "gookism" in the Vietnam War. According to Asian American movement scholar William Wei, the term was first used during the Philippine-American War (1899–1902) to name Filipinos with no mix of European heritage. Later "the appellation has been applied to Haitians, Nicaraguans, Costa Ricans, and other people of color, but since the Korean War it has been used mainly by U.S. soldiers to denigrate Asian people. It implied that they were in the Vietnam War to prepare soldiers to psychologically maim and kill Southeast Asians, according to some Asian American veterans" (38). "Gookism" encouraged a psychology of racism and racial violence, but the increasing popularity of "gookism" in the late 1960s helped awaken an Asian American critical consciousness.

With this memory of "gookism," we are left with a troubling understanding of McCain's utterance. As Duc explained: "We can't allow a public figure, any public figures, anybody that has influence upon people to use that kind of language, to use the term 'gook' so casually. *And* to convince our community that 'gook' equals 'communist' because it does not." He was concerned that a public figure's use of a racial slur could perpetuate ongoing normalization of racializing language. Largely ignoring the memories of Vietnamese Americans and other Asian Americans, Duc argued, would harm our communities, aggravating the anger, violence, and dehumanization of Asian Americans. Indeed, he was not alone. In the March 5, 2000, issue of the *New York Times*, journalist Anthony Ramirez wrote that the controversy "flared and faded within a few days," but critiques of McCain's statement continued online. For instance, in his article Ramirez quoted Jocelyn Dong's post to an Asian American journalists forum: "The English language is rife with words to express a former POW's feelings toward the men who tortured him . . . [b]ut the slur he's sticking to is the racial one. Not one that zeroes in on the unconscionable cruelty of his enemies, but one that expresses hatred of 'differentness'—skin color, facial features, culture."

Duc's protest against McCain's utterance teaches us that rhetorical memory can account for how the memorial sign had recurred within plural contextual memories and how writers and speakers frame signs within these contexts. Imploring his peers to take action, Duc juxtaposed copious memorial traces that decentered McCain and McCain's part in authorizing harmful conceptions of Asian Americans. This composition traversed memorial sites that are significant to historical processes of Asian American racial formation: McCain's statements on the 2000 campaign trail; the internally conflicted Little Saigon community; racial hate crimes against Vincent Chin and Thien Minh Ly; racialization during the Vietnam War; *and* the university site where Duc persuaded his peers to act. Importantly, the memorial traces did not cancel one another. Their simultaneous part in the composition worked to destabilize the primacy of any one memory. At the nexus of student activists and a prominent politician, bullhorns and mass media, grassroots protest and electoral politics, this case of Asian American rhetorical memory makes palpable memory's inseparability from ideological and social concerns. What divided McCain's perspective from the Asian American protester's perspective was not necessarily the simple question of whose memory was "right"; rather, the protest happened because of struggles over memorial entitlement and conflicts between their understandings of memory as representational or rhetorical.

As important as these memorial investigations were to recasting Mc-Cain's reference to "gooks," what mattered most to Duc was engaging the Vietnamese American community. Reflecting on the protest, he told me, "We were there to educate them." Whereas Duc began discussing the protest by focusing on the argument he offered to his peers in the Vietnamese American Coalition, he then turned my attention to the dramatic events of the protest. In addition to employing copia through his memorial investigation of the word "gook," he now employed copia by reframing the event in plural ways, each time calling attention to social interaction. His first account of the protest is framed by a conversation with his student organization and located at an educational site. His copious recounting continues with multiple frames and thus takes us to three other cultural sites of memory, all off-stage: the protest site in Little Saigon; the site of the activists' discourse community; and the street-side contact zone of activists, opponents of the activists, and the police. These memorial reframings and Duc's movement among the cultural sites highlight the importance that he placed on social engagement and shared cultural production with his audience.

Duc's memorial account traveled to a different cultural site with each reframing, first as the persuasive dialogue with fellow VAC students discussed earlier. Drawing on the same memorial premises, he then reframed the narrative as a persuasive speech event in the Little Saigon rally:

> I spoke in Vietnamese on the, on the bullhorn . . . to the people at the rally, and I was explaining it to them in Vietnamese. I was saying how this term is unacceptable, how terms like this lead to hate crimes and murders, and I brought up Thien Minh Ly. I brought up how people can't tell the difference between a Vietnamese commie, or, or VC, and you or I.
>
> They were listening. They were listening. And we were rallying, too. I got, I got the bullhorn, and I was like, "Are you a gook?" to those people who were there to support McCain. And they were actually on our side. You know, we were rallying, you know?

Moving from the first site of the university student organization, Duc called attention to the protest site as a dynamic engagement. With the university site, he spent relatively more time arguing about investigating "gook" as a memorial sign, and he framed all this with an explanation of VAC officers' need for politicization. By contrast, with the protest site, Duc spent relatively less time on the premises of his argument and more time on the audience's participation. By stressing he was speaking Vietnamese in the excerpt above and several other moments in the interview and by stressing the audience's involvement, Duc emphasized that his argument was not directed at McCain so much as it was directed at the Vietnamese community who had shown up in support of McCain. He was encouraged by community members' support for the protesters' efforts, being informed of what McCain had said and being persuaded that it was harmful. We experience not just a shift in our lens but a shift in audience.

Duc then moves us *within* the discourse community of his fellow Asian American activists when recalling a conversation he had with a disillusioned friend: "And another thing I remember from that was a friend of mine—. Everyone was really upset at the reaction from the comm-, at the reaction from the people who were Vietnamese American who went to rally in support of McCain. And one of my friends got so upset, and he, he was telling me that we just need to wait until they, being older Vietnamese Americans who don't understand or whatever, to die. And I was like, 'My God.'" Here, Duc turned away from his audience to a fellow protester, distracted by his friend's missing the point of engaging the community. The friend, he told me, believed that only when the first-generation Vietnamese Americans—those who support McCain and continue to resent communists—die out will the entire community progress. Duc's response is telling: "That made me very angry. That made me extremely angry. And I was trying to tell him, 'No. That's not it.' Because we were there to educate them, you know? We were there to educate the community. We didn't know the media was going to be, like, swarming around us."

Through these triply reframed accounts, we understand the multiple participants involved in this event: Duc and other activists, VAC student leaders, Vietnamese American community members, and a disillusioned friend. McCain, in fact, has little agency in these accounts and retreats into the background of Duc's telling. What mattered most to Duc was building solidarity with the Vietnamese American community. The focus on off-stage cultural sites decenters McCain's onstage presence, suggesting that Duc was more interested in community activism *for* the community rather than *against* McCain. For Duc, the protest was about the social effect of McCain's "gook" utterance. The community members present could respond in at least two ways: McCain and his audience would read "gook" as something innocuous, what a patriotic war hero and political authority had uttered. Or community members could recognize that Duc and fellow activists meant to foster social involvement, a dialogue between themselves and the Vietnamese community, to claim agency over the memorial sign of "gook" and its historical resonance.

Duc urged that Asian and Asian Americans had historically been tangled up in "gookism," and he was trying to share the memorial traces of "gookism" with the ethnic community. As philosopher Avishai Margalit has aptly explained: "The significance of the event for us depends on our being personally connected with what happened, and hence we share not only the memory of what happened but also our participation in it" (53). In this sense, Duc aimed to increase community members' participation in claiming agency over "gook" as a sign with a memory. These ideas came to a head in the final cultural site within his account: a contact zone among Duc and fellow activists, opponents of the activists, and police.

In a dramatic conflict between Duc and an audience member who opposed the activist stance of the Asian American students, memory became a cultural affair where Duc's purpose was to have the community jointly call attention to the harmfulness of the term "gook." Duc explained that some opposition in the audience had started calling him and fellow protesters "communists" with the rationale that if they were opposing McCain, a former prisoner-of-war, they must be communists. With the protest taking place in the commercial center of Little Saigon, where people had fled because of North Vietnamese persecution and violence, the allegation of being "commies" had heavy consequences. The crowd became violent, pushing the protesters into oncoming traffic. As Duc tells it:

Duc: All of a sudden, it became a whole crowd of people. I don't know h—. All of a sudden, just instantly. They started *pushing* us. And then, like, a lot of my friends kind of protected me as I continued to speak. (laughs) And . . . and I was continuing my little spiel.

Yeah, and then we started chanting, you know. And then they continued to push us. And they poked us and they pinched us and people spat on us and they threw stuff at us. And they pushed us onto oncoming traffic on Bolsa Avenue.

And at the same time, while that was all happening—When we first started rallying, you know, all the cameras are pointed onto the stage, onto that media press thing up high, I guess bleachers or whatever. . . .

And all of the cameras turned around. And all of a sudden, it was a mixture of people poking us and spitting on us and throwing stuff at us and yelling at us and saying we were commies and going like that (shoots an angry stare).

HH: In English or in Vietnamese?

Duc: In Vietnamese *and* in English. I spoke in English, too. And we weren't all Vietnamese Americans, you know. There were Japanese Americans, Filipino Americans, you know. There were Chinese Americans.

HH: Mostly college students?

Duc: Yeah, mostly students from [the university]. And a lot of people I didn't even know who got the flyer and, "Hey, you know, totally, we'll be out there," and whatever. And they showed up. And they pushed, they pushed all of us. Some guy got arrested for, he was running, running at me to knock me over, whatever. He didn't get me, but a cop arrested him. And then we started chanting, "Do not arrest him."

HH: Why is that?

Duc: My reason was he just didn't understand. He was my same age, you know, and we could easily talk to him and he could easily understand us and easily identify why we shouldn't allow McCain to use this word or to be unapologetic about using it.

Despite the fact that a man was charging Duc, he remained steadfast in his intention to communicate with rather than defeat those who disagreed with his stance.

In this cultural site of memory, the police, though trying to protect the activists, indicate the challenges of memorial production within social structure. The police function to impose discipline, a paradigm that could not account for Duc's hope for an opening, a space to deliberately compose memory. The shifts among the cultural sites of memory—university, Little Saigon protest, activist community, and the policed society—present the complexity of Asian American memorial production within social conditions. Moreover, when Duc's recollection moves among these sites of memory, he underscores his attention to social engagement. The protest did receive brief media attention, but its departure from news accounts was quick. In any case, Duc explained that the point of the protest was to engage fellow Asian Americans in the making of memories, to compose more textured and socially responsible American cultural memories; he did not anticipate the media attention. Bringing up memory was a way of inviting participation, involvement, and solidarity among the Vietnamese and Vietnamese American community. The struggle here was about Vietnamese American and other Asian American student activists literally placing their memorial practices center stage, where only silenced memories and McCain's racial epithet had previously been recognized.

TOWARD A "DELIBERATE ACT OF REMEMBERING"

Defining an Asian American rhetorical memory requires a deep analysis of sites where Asian Americans have refashioned memory in response to histories, representations, and experiences. The "American

Gook" protest and other performances of Asian American rhetorical memory suggest that the rhetorical *art* of memory is wedded to the social conditions in which that art is practiced. Asian American rhetorical memory thus entails investigating the memory traces that emerge from Asian American cultural sites. In composing Asian American memory, writers and speakers contribute to an American cultural production. Margalit has described this social involvement in memory as a mnemonic division of labor, where what is important is not just the memorial referent but participation in the memorial activity (51–53). Memory, then, is not just about legitimated recovery of marginalized experiences. Rather, rhetorical memory is a process of participation in a wider cultural production. Toni Morrison's reflections on her writing capture this sentiment:

> My compact with the reader is not to reveal an already established reality (literary or historical) that he or she and I agree with beforehand. I don't want to assume or exercise that kind of authority. I regard that as patronizing, although many people regard it as safe and reassuring. And because my métier is Black, the artistic demands of Black culture are such that I cannot patronize, control, or pontificate. In the Third World cosmology as I perceive it, reality is not already constituted by my literary predecessors in Western culture. If my work is to confront a reality of the West, it must centralize and animate information discredited by the west—discredited not because it is not true or useful or even of some racial value, but because it is information held by discredited people, information dismissed as "lore" or "gossip" or "magic" or "sentiment." (388)

In the "American Gook" protest Duc's purpose also went against this kind of "patronizing"—an attitude reflected in the disillusioned student's comments that they should wait until the older oppositional generation died. He composed memories to invite further memorial production, significant for social engagement, thereby working toward copia and destabilizing cultural production. And because each community member's memory is necessarily partial, such participation in memory presumes a spirit of cooperation and provisional memory work.

Reviving the art of memory matters: memory is a complex art that entails critically interpreting a sign's past and varied utterances, selectively weaving memorial compositions, and sharing cultural memories to foster social engagement. Asian American rhetorical memory, in particular, reveals how intricate layers of cultural memories are re-collected into compositions and how the textured meanings that emerge from this copia foster social involvement and community solidarity.

When rhetorical memory disappears, we should be wary. As rhetorician Kathleen Welch has warned, "It is crucial to an understanding of Western literacy at this millennium to recognize that the disappearance of memory and delivery is not a benign removal; rather, it is part of a larger movement in the United States to pablumize the humanities in general and to vitiate writing in particular by behaving as if it were a mere skill, craft, or useful tool" (18). For Asian Americans, who are so often disregarded by mainstream American history, making our own memories is a critical answer to compositionists Jacqueline Jones Royster and Jean C. Williams's call to write in the "spaces left" and to resist the primacy of officialized narratives. By no means are the Asian American activists' memorial acts at the McCain protest representative of all Asian Americans, but this instance of rhetorical memory does point to the challenge broadly faced by Asian American rhetorical memory: to strategically construct collective identity, challenge racial injustice, and generally participate in American civic life.

Chapter 5

"I WANT A THICKER ACCENT"
Revisionary Public Texts

i tell you all this
to fill the void of absence
in our history
here
. . .
let people know
VIETNAM IS NOT A WAR
let people know
VIETNAM IS NOT A WAR
let people know
VIETNAM IS NOT A WAR
but a piece of
us,
sister
and we are
so much
more

—Le Thi Diem Thuy, excerpt from "Shrapnel Shards on Blue Water"
(qtd. in Vietnamese American Curriculum Project Committee 161–62)

The resignification of speech requires opening new contexts, speaking in ways
that have never yet been legitimated, and hence producing legitimation in new
and future forms.
—Judith Butler, Excitable Speech: The Politics of Performativity, 41

In spring 2002, students in the Vietnamese American Coalition (VAC)
created public texts that performed and revised their ethnic, racial, and
gendered identities. That April, the Orange County Asian Pacific Islander Community Alliance (OCAPICA), whose former associate director had cofounded VAC nine years earlier, held a press conference
for a new Vietnamese American social science curriculum for middle
and high school students. In May VAC's sister student organization put
on a Culture Night performance, authored by a VAC student, to an au-

dience of over a thousand students, alumni, and friends. And as the quarter rounded to a close in June, two VAC students and classmates from their performance art course produced and performed in a show, and another VAC student posted textual art stating "I LOVE YOUR ACCENT" and "I WANT A THICKER ACCENT" around the fine arts corner of campus. VAC students' texts tugged at their identities and opened up possibilities for what I see as a transformative Asian American rhetoric.

Performative public texts represent the deliberate culmination of strategies to recall (and perhaps rewrite) Asian American subject positions. By calling these public texts "performative"—speech and writing that *do* rather than *report* something—I suggest that race consciousness is not rigid and something already acquired but must be repeatedly performed. As I explore the relationship between performativity and race, I begin with sociolinguist J. L. Austin's introduction of performatives into speech act theory and then turn quickly to feminist theorist Judith Butler's extension of performativity as critical theory. Butler's valuable claim that utterances *perform* (rather than *express*) gendered identity enables me to unravel how Vietnamese American public texts have shaped and reshaped *ethnic* and *racial* identities. These public texts, as this chapter's epigraphs suggest, "open new contexts" to legitimate constructions of Vietnam and Vietnamese Americans as "so much more" than a war.

PERFORMATIVITY: FROM *HOW TO DO THINGS WITH WORDS* TO SUBVERSIVE PERFORMATIVES

J. L. Austin's widely influential 1962 *How To Do Things with Words* has challenged the category of true-false (or constative) statements and proposed the category of performative acts "in which to *say* something is to *do* something" (12). Take his classic examples: "'I do (sc. take this woman to be my lawful wedded wife)'—as in the course of the marriage ceremony" and "'I bet you sixpence it will rain tomorrow,'" where "I do" and "I bet" enact a state of affairs that do not refer to something beyond the immediate speech situation (5). Austin reconceives of language as an act rather than a mirror and thus sets about articulating what is now known as speech act theory. Considering the difficulty of distinguishing between constative and performative statements, Austin eventually determines that while the constative calls attention to the utterance's referential act (or locutionary act) and the performative highlights the utterance's force (or illocutionary act), "every genuine speech act is both" (146). In fact, "we must consider the total situation in which the utterance is issued—the total speech-act—if we are to see the parallel between [constative] statements and performative utterances, and how each can go wrong. Perhaps indeed there is no great distinction between statements and performative utterances" (52). Furthermore, we may judge speech acts according to the "doctrine of infelicities." That is, we cannot talk about performatives as true or false but rather as happy or unhappy. The felicitous-infelicitous doctrine calls on us to ask what would make VAC students' performatives felicitous. For Austin, a happy performative relies on the invocation and execution of performative discourse conventions by appropriate participants. The individuals in a wedding ceremony, for instance, must be authorized and willing to participate in a conventional ceremony for the performative to succeed. Even if such conventional circumstances were not observed, the speaker's utterance would still be performative; only, it may be an unhappy performative. These circumstances, Austin elaborates, must be considered in light of the "total speech-act."

What defines the "total speech-act" becomes a pivotal question for Judith Butler as she takes our inquiry into performativity from speech act theory to postmodern critical theory. With a deft turn, Butler revises Austin's proposal that we "do things with words" to say that words themselves *do* things; words are "transitive" rather than "instrumental." Butler, contends that the total speech act goes beyond the immediate situation because a single utterance calls up iterations of that performative: "The illocutionary speech act performs its deed *at the moment* of the utterance, and yet to the extent that the moment is ritualized, it is never merely a single moment" (*Excitable Speech* 3). Butler's attention to repetition is fundamental to her seminal studies of gendered identity as well as hate speech. Signs perform and constitute identity, and the repetition of these signs authorizes particular constructions of gender and racial identity. Identity, then, does not refer to an authentic self—in this chapter, an authentic Vietnamese American identity—but rather an intertextual web of preceding constructions of identity. It is for this reason that Senator John McCain's utterance of the racial slur "gook," discussed in chapter 4, was offensive to student activists. Even though he directed his attack at the North Vietnamese military, McCain's utterance was not singular but carried the weight of preceding inflections of the word.

As much as repeated constructions of identity often limit women and minorities, Butler finds hope in the potential for repetition with *variation*: "Agency is the hiatus in iterability, the compulsion to install an identity through repetition, which requires the very contingency, the undetermined interval, that identity insistently seeks to foreclose. . . . [T]he future of the signifier of identity can only be secured through a repetition that fails to repeat loyally, a reciting of the signifier that must commit a disloyalty against identity" (*Bodies That Matter* 220). Since each iteration is its own performance, there is the potential to resignify the iteration in a new context. In this sense, the student activists who opposed McCain's utterance introduced a "hiatus" to the slur's repetition and re-performed the signifier by ironically writing "American Gook" on their T-shirts, perhaps implying that the utterance hurts *Americans*.

I call attention to such agency in the public texts circulating among and created by VAC students. By recollecting and composing public texts, VAC students and other Vietnamese Americans could interrupt limited iterations of their identity. Public texts potentially introduce identities contingent on sociohistorical conditions that subvert earlier constructions of identity as universal. Drawing from critical theorist Slavoj Žižek, Butler explains that this effort to authorize a revised identity creates a "temporary linguistic unity," a short halting of the repetition, so as to create solidarity (*Bodies That Matter* 220). Performativity thereby enables marginalized people to exert agency over their identity and play a fundamental role in the ongoing repetitions, subversions, and reauthorizations of identities.

"AND WE ARE SO MUCH MORE": A VIETNAMESE AMERICAN CURRICULUM

On April 20, 2002, the Orange County Asian Pacific Islander Community Alliance (OCAPICA), a community health and education nonprofit organization, invited news media and local Vietnamese community members to the official press release of a Vietnamese American curriculum. A curriculum committee consisting of local community members (teachers, a graduate student, a foundation grant maker, the director of OCAPICA) produced a curriculum meant to supplement middle and high school students' social science and language arts learning. Le's poem "Shrapnel Shards on Blue Water," cited in the epigraph and included in the curriculum, crystallizes the public text's performative dimension. After recounting memories to her sister about how their parents, "ma" and "ba," had worked for the family's survival, the poet expresses to her sister a hunger for history that risks being erased. She closes the poem with simple but poignant lines:

> let people know
> VIETNAM IS NOT A WAR
> but a piece of
> us,
> sister

and we are
so much
more

In recounting personal and collective experiences of Vietnamese people in the United States, the curriculum titled *Vietnamese Americans: Lessons in American History, An Interdisciplinary Curriculum and Resource Guide* evidences performative acts in public texts as well as the balance between authority and revision that felicitous performatives require.

An Overview of *Vietnamese Americans: Lessons in American History*

One week before the press release, Bryan, the 2001–2002 VAC chair and an OCAPICA intern, invited me to an OCAPICA meeting for press conference preparations. The committee generously offered me a copy of the curriculum when they heard about my interest in VAC and Vietnamese American students. *Lessons in American History* begins with a preface that explains the purpose of the curriculum, "What does it mean to be 'Vietnamese American?' How is this different from being 'Vietnamese,' from being 'American,' and from being 'American Vietnamese'? This Vietnamese American curriculum guide does not attempt to definitively answer these questions, but rather it hopes to shed light on the complexities of such an identity group, while bridging cultural gaps with more awareness of shared experiences" (Vietnamese American Curriculum Project Committee vii).

The preface opens into eight sections:

Historical Overview

Timelines

Maps and Demographics

Lesson Plans

Primary Sources

Glossary

Bibliography

Resources

In the first sections of the curriculum, readers find background information about the immigration experiences and social circumstances surrounding Vietnamese people's immigration to the United States. An excerpt from Min Zhou and Carl L. Bankston's *Straddling Two Social Worlds: The Experience of Vietnamese Refugee Children in the United*

States reviews the displacement of Vietnamese refugees to the United States, reporting numbers of refugees and later immigrants, major waves of immigration, and U.S. public policy that has affected Vietnamese refugees (qtd in Vietnamese American Curriculum Project Committee). Next, timelines list major political events in Vietnam, among Vietnamese in America, and among Vietnamese in Orange County. The latter two timelines report a range of events: President Clinton's normalizing diplomatic relations with Vietnam; incidents of hate crime; actor Dustin Nguyễn's starring role on the television show *21 Jump Street*; and the National Football League's first Vietnamese American player Đạt Nguyễn. A third section summarizes demographic and geographic information about Vietnamese Americans and Vietnam.

Following these sociohistorical sections, we come upon what the editors call the central part of the curriculum, the lesson plans:

The Boat People: Separation and Loss

Immigrants and Refugees

Voice and Identity

Hate Crimes

Human Rights

Ho Chi Minh and Freedom of Speech

Oral History and Multiculturalism

A Vietnamese American Monument

Supplemental Activities in Multiculturalism and Human Relations

These lessons introduce teachers, who would in turn introduce students, to issues of social displacement, identity formation, and civil rights. Drawing from recent news stories and narratives of personal experience, student readings touch on various topics, including immigration policy, the brutal hate crime against Thien Minh Ly, community protests against a Little Saigon business owner who proudly displayed Vietnam's current national flag, human rights violations in Vietnam, and oral histories of Vietnamese survivors of the Vietnam War. Supplementing these lesson plans, the next section includes original poems, short stories, and oral histories. The curriculum ends with a bibliography and list of community resources (nonprofit organizations, libraries, politicians, and media websites) meant to support further study.

The Vietnamese American Curriculum as Performative

Lessons in American History does not simply *report* history but *makes* history through the reporting. First addressing the curriculum as *con-*

stative—that is, as making our history more comprehensive and therefore more "true"—the editors of the curriculum assert that K–12 education has neglected a major thread of American history and culture. In an article that appears in *Amerasia Journal*'s special issue on "Vietnamese Americans: Diaspora and Dimensions," several editors persuasively argue for the urgency in implementing curricula that address Asian Pacific American experiences.

Across the United States, there is a gaping silence in state content standards for K–12: "In California, the state with the largest API [Asian Pacific Islander] population, the only mention of APIs in the California Content Standards for the Social Studies from seventh through twelfth grades—the extensive document adhered to by all public schools statewide—is in the case of the forced internment of Japanese Americans during World War II" (Beevi, Lam, and Matsuda 166). American histories that neglect Asian Pacific American experiences, particularly those histories authorized by schools, also bear a *performative* force, constructing and perpetuating a limited Asian Pacific American identity. When the only Asian Pacific Americans included in K–12 curricula are Japanese American and they are depicted only in the context of war and as potential enemies and perpetual foreigners, we face a history that is not just deeply partial but also harmful. Add to this the string of cultural stereotypes running through films and news media—for instance, Vietnam War films that "include sadistic Viet Cong soldiers, helpless villagers, and desperate prostitutes"—and the need to revise cultural representations becomes even more pressing (167). Rather than inviting Vietnamese American students to conceive of themselves as part of a larger American history, rather than asking other American students to identify and reconstruct American history, such curricula are acts of disidentification.

Lessons in American History was a response to this problem. In an interview, Bryan brought up the curriculum and the more general need for Vietnamese American representation in K–12 education:

> Being able to look at what we learn in the educational system is important. Is it reflective of our communities? Is that what *we* want to teach other people that, say, aren't Vietnamese? Is that what we want to be known for? The war? Is that it? Within high school, when you think about history, you learn— If you're not Vietnamese, then what you learn about Vietnamese is that they're poor people, they're a product of the war. We're more than that. Like any other ethnic group, you know? So, having a say in education, like in the curriculum with which we learn. Both levels, high school as well as college. Even earlier. That's one issue.

The curriculum was a collective effort to revise school versions of our histories and our identities. A collaborative project, the curriculum was created by the Vietnamese American Curriculum Project Committee, primarily made up of volunteers—including Michael, the former OCAPICA associate director and one of VAC's cofounders. Michael had worked to start up OCAPICA after receiving his master's in public policy from Harvard's John F. Kennedy School of Government. The curriculum committee, an OCAPICA initiative, was further assisted by current VAC students: Bryan, who interned for the nonprofit, and Duc, who contributed signage for the event. Together, the committee's collaborative authorship, appeal for community approval, and efforts to garner media attention indicate the committee's awareness of the curriculum's sociohistorical context and the text's potential to revise constructions of Vietnamese American history and culture.

This rhetorical consciousness, in fact, influenced the committee's distribution and subsequent revisions to the curriculum. From drafting to revising and later publicizing the curriculum, the editors continually invited others to respond to the curriculum. In March and April of 2001, after drafting the curriculum with the help of an Orange County Human Relations Commission grant, the curriculum committee piloted several lesson plans with students at one local high school and also with students in an inter-high-school Vietnamese student organization. In May the committee held a training workshop for twenty-seven teachers in the Anaheim Union High School District, where 12 to 15 percent of the student body at that time was of Asian Pacific Islander heritage. After their discussions with students and teachers, the editors made revisions over the next four months that "incorporate[d] feedback from students, teachers, and other outside evaluators" (Beevi, Lam, and Matsuda 168–69). By summer, the local newspaper, *Việt Tide*, printed the headline "Making, Teaching History," reporting that the curriculum committee was working with educators at the Anaheim Union High School District to pilot the curriculum (Phan).

"Our next step," the editors wrote, "was to get the word out to the local schools, the communities, and the public and political officials about the critical content and importance of *Lessons in American History*, and its potential impact on students' personal and intellectual growth" (Beevi, Lam, and Matsuda 169). Attuned to the curriculum's potential reach, the curriculum committee was conscientious about appealing to and identifying with the public media, educators, and other concerned citizens. On April 20, 2002, OCAPICA held a press release in the conference room of a local major Vietnamese newspaper called *Người Việt*. In Little Saigon most who attended the press release were journalists from local mainstream and Vietnamese news media as well as Vietnamese and Vietnamese American community members. With these multiple audiences, the press release speeches about the curriculum and the curriculum itself became multivalent sources for identification, where the editors asked audiences to identify with the curriculum's reconstruction of cultural memory. The first-generation, culturally conservative Vietnamese community identified with the preservation of culture, the persistent attention to human rights violations in Vietnam, and the desire for their children to connect with their generation. Also appealing to Vietnamese Americans, including VAC students and myself, the curriculum committee introduced cultural pride, identity formation in the United States, and struggles for civil liberties. In the few days before and after the press release, articles reporting on and affirming the curriculum appeared in several local Vietnamese newspapers: *Việt Báo Daily News*, *Người Việt*, and *Viễn Đông Daily News*.

More broadly, the curriculum's editors identified with the general American public, especially necessary because the committee hoped that the curriculum would transform schools across the nation. The morning of the press release, in the local section of the *Orange County Register*, journalist Katherine Nguyen's article "Guide on Vietnamese Experience to Debut" reported on the day's events. After announcing the press conference and briefly summarizing the curriculum's key points, the article closes with summary comments from one of the curriculum editors (not associated with VAC):

> "When teachers teach their students about First Amendment–rights issues, they can refer to the Little Saigon protests," said Michael Matsuda, a teacher in the Anaheim Union High School District and chairman of the Orange County Asian and Pacific Islander Community Alliance, which gave $20,000 to print 500 copies of the curriculum.
>
> About a dozen educators and community leaders collaborated for over a year to design the lesson plan.
>
> Matsuda and alliance members said they hope teachers across the county will incorporate the material into classroom lessons.
>
> "The story of the Vietnamese (in America) is universal, like the Italians or the Jews," Matsuda said. "They are stories of survival and growth and need to be acknowledged as part of the American mosaic."

Here, Matsuda aligned Vietnamese American experiences with Italian and Jewish people who have immigrated to the United States; those on the Mayflower were "boat people" just like Vietnamese Americans, he asserted (and Bryan later echoed in a VAC meeting). Given his role in editing and writing a curriculum grounded in Vietnamese American history, Matsuda surely understood that he was making simple comparisons of disparate immigrant groups, and he makes these identifications, I believe, to achieve mutual recognition.

In the preface of *Lessons in American History*, for instance, the editors invite readers to consider the curriculum as part of the American experience:

> We hope that this curriculum will inform teachers and students about some of the important experiences of the Vietnamese American community today, so that we can better understand and value the complexities of this group of Americans. These Vietnamese American experiences, however, are only one part of the richly textured American fabric. We hope that this curriculum will launch future curricula about other equally important, but often neglected, communities that make up the United States. Only by including instruction on these groups in schools and by promoting knowledge of the experiences and contributions of diverse communities can we begin to teach tolerance, acceptance, empathy, and appreciation of the unique tapestry that is America. (Vietnamese American Curriculum Project Committee xi)

The "unique tapestry that is America" becomes a repeated source for identification, difficult to reject because to learn about Vietnamese Americans is to become more knowledgeable about Americans. The title of the curriculum echoes that it offers lessons in *American* history, not solely *Vietnamese* American history, thereby resignifying or at least asking readers to question what it means to "be American." Matsuda's appeal to multiple audiences and multiple histories is a re-membering of American history, both a recollection and a re-peopling.

The curriculum is thus "making history" in two senses. In the more common idiomatic sense, "making history" means putting forth an innovation. Local newspapers introduced the curriculum as the first of its kind, an educational supplement that could enrich current education about American history and culture. But the curriculum also literally *makes* history, constituting Vietnamese American cultural memory and identity and, moreover, American cultural memory and identity. "The signifiers of 'identity' effectively or rhetorically produce the very social movements that they appear to represent," Butler has written. "The signifier does not refer to a pregiven or already constituted identity, a pure referent or essential set of facts that preexist the identity-signifier or act as the measure of its adequacy" (*Bodies That Matter* 210). The challenge that the curriculum committee and teachers face when identifying with a shared American identity lies in the precarious balance between using contingent Vietnamese American experiences to revise American identity, on the one hand, and subsuming Vietnamese

American experiences under already prevalent constructions of Americanness, on the other.

Felicitous Performativity: Authority and Revision

For the curriculum to be *happy* performatives, readers must accept that America is diverse and that curricula, identities, and histories can be revised. The editors of the curriculum explain:

> Since this guide is also an attempt to encourage students to recognize and appreciate differences and commonalities between various groups, it hopes to explore the complexities and limitations of the designation "Vietnamese American." Given the pervasive, racialized perception of Asian Americans as foreigners and model minorities, "Asian American" and "Vietnamese American" as political markers are often excluded from the usual public discourse on race and from discussions on and considerations of social policy formation. The community's experiences and struggles should ideally be considered alongside those of African Americans, Chicanos/Latinos, and Native Americans, Pacific Islanders and other Asian Americans. (Vietnamese American Curriculum Project Committee viii)

Constructing a plural America means placing side-by-side the particular experiences of multiple groups (African American, Chicanos/Latinos, Native Americans, and Pacific Islanders and other Asian Americans) and never growing satisfied with any of these "identity" signifiers.

But who has the power to revise Vietnamese American and, more generally, American narratives? A second condition required for a performative text's felicity is the authority to perform revisions to dominant constructions of American identity. The curriculum committee certainly has a strong ethos; collectively the authors, including VAC's cofounder, have intensive education and experience with teaching, community action, and public policy. However, Butler suggests that authors only bear a small proportion of power when she persuasively counters Austin's presumption of the speaker's inherent authority: "If a performative provisionally succeeds (and I will suggest that 'success' is always and only provisional), then it is not because intention successfully governs the action of speech, but only because that act echoes prior actions, and *accumulates the force of authority through the repetition or citation of a prior and authoritative set of practices*" (*Excitable Speech* 51). The authority to revise American history and identity reaches beyond the immediate speech act and into the utterance's "historicity of force" (51).

Because the curriculum is the first of its kind and is "making history," then it cannot rely on its own prior repetition but the repetition of that which it revises: mainstream curricula that have neglected Asian Pacific American experiences. By identifying with school discourse conventions, *Lessons in American History* asserts the authority to revise curricular content. The curriculum mirrors the conventional organization of school discourse: historical overviews, timelines, lesson plans with secondary and primary sources followed by questions, and resources for further research. The editors call attention to the few but important precedents set by similar curricula, including the Japanese American Citizens League's *A Lesson in American History: The Japanese American Experience* and the California Heritage Pilot Project directed at the Chinese American experiences (cited in Beevi, Lam, and Matsuda 166–67). Finally, the curriculum is also authorized by those who promote and distribute it. The curriculum was widely circulated in Orange County—the teachers who served on the curriculum committee were important to this distribution. What is important here are the people and organizations that sponsor the curriculum: the Anaheim Union High School District, a local university that offers training workshops for implementing the curriculum, and, more recently, the Southern Poverty Law Center's web project "Fight Hate and Promote Tolerance." The Southern Poverty Law Center, in purchasing the right to distribute the curriculum online, grants the curriculum more authority with progressive educators and other citizens who challenge racism and discrimination.

But there is still the risk that what was intended to be a revised and even subversive curriculum could simply replace the old dominant construction of "American" with another dominant construction. As Butler has explained, any construction of identity—whether gendered, Vietnamese American, or American—is always provisional; the construction has no true referent and therefore the referent is the "site of impossible desire" (*Bodies That Matter* 219).

Not only was identity performed between the curriculum committee and general public and between educators and students; the curriculum also asks students to talk back to the public. The lessons ask students to identify with the issues raised by Vietnamese American experiences, such as displacement, freedom of speech, and human rights violations, but they also call on students to revise what is already in the lessons' texts. The lesson on hate crimes, for instance, has students write a "Personal Action Plan" to combat racism (Vietnamese American Curriculum Project Committee 68–71). When students read about human rights violations in Vietnam, they are to write letters to [then current] President George W. Bush recommending action (88–89). After reading the oral history of a South Vietnamese soldier about his experiences in a reeducation camp, where he went from 165 pounds to 88 pounds, students are to write narratives from their own oral history interviews (112–21). In these lessons students do the work of revising cultural representations and identity, of making history.

Lessons in American History responds to two pointed questions that Butler has raised about identification and solidarity: "What are the possibilities of politicizing *dis*identification, this experience of *misrecognition*, this uneasy sense of standing under a sign to which one does and does not belong? And how are we to interpret this disidentification produced by and through the very signifier that holds out the promise of solidarity?" (*Bodies That Matter* 219). The curriculum committee steps into a moment of disidentification with mainstream middle and high school social studies curricula, revising the source of that disidentification. As Butler has suggested, the recognition that identity is performed and then authorized through repetition opens a space for democratic revision of that identity. The curriculum as a public text uses this space to re-perform American history, cultural representations, and identity among the general public, educators, and students and, in doing so, again holds out the promise of solidarity. This solidarity is one that is based on a collaboratively constructed cultural memory of Vietnamese American experiences. What we learn from the performativity of this curriculum is that such solidarity is temporary and vibrant, awaiting and even encouraging yet another performance.

Re-Presentations of Vietnamese American Women in a Culture Night Performance

Every year, Vietnamese and Vietnamese American Culture Nights take place at many U.S. universities during the month of May, Asian American Heritage Month. Culture Night performances are mixed-genre celebrations of culture, typically framed by a play but also including a range of traditional and contemporary dance, song, and fashion shows. In June 2002, the student production involved a team of dedicated volunteers not from VAC but from its sister student organization, the Vietnamese Student Association (VSA). While VAC students work toward political and community activism, VSA students direct their efforts toward cultural and social events like Culture Night. The fact that four of the twelve 2001–2002 VAC students I interviewed contributed to the VSA Culture Night—as writer, actor, dancer, and fundraiser—and that all twelve attended the event speaks to VAC students' commitment to cultural heritage in addition to political activism.

In 2002 William, an active member in VAC *and* VSA, wrote the play *What Dreams May Come* for that year's Culture Night at the university.

What Culture Nights demonstrate is that perform*ance* is potentially perform*ative* in terms of constituting (not expressing) ethnic identity and cultural memories. *What Dreams May Come*, in particular, reconstitutes Vietnamese American cultural memories by stressing the centrality of intergenerational, familial relationships—specifically, grandmother-mother-daughter relationships—as part of who we are. *What Dreams May Come* was performed on May 11, 2002, before several hundred, if not more than a thousand, students, alumni, family, and other community members. The play, which knits lighthearted humor with drama, opens with the birth of My Anh in a scene titled "1925 The Birth of New Hopes and Dreams." Taking more of an epic than narrative form, the three acts each move through a quarter of a century and follow three generations of women through struggle and survival. In Act I we meet the baby girl My Anh, whose birth is marked by social pressures when her father comically seeks out a priest and then a monk's blessing for the son he wishes to have. When her parents face dire economic circumstances, they send My Anh to live with her older sister Nga in Hanoi. Distressed, My Anh's mother gives My Anh a book to remember her by. As the years pass, My Anh grows up to become an intelligent young woman and soon falls in love with Quan, who is a busboy but tells My Anh that he is studying to become a doctor. My Anh eventually learns that Quan is not a medical student but a secret agent working for the U.S. government and against the French and Japanese military. Meanwhile, Nga's internalized colonial sensibility leads her to hold the French in higher esteem than the Vietnamese. She therefore disapproves of Quan and disowns My Anh when they ask for Nga's blessing on their marriage.

In Act II we follow My Anh and Quan to their first apartment, where they raise their only daughter, Uyen. The characters' lives are punctuated by increasing political turmoil: My Anh realizes that Quan has worked as an American spy against the French and Japanese; Japanese forces retreat from Vietnam; and finally the French colonial rule also departs from Vietnam. As the family migrates south to Saigon in 1950, we turn to the next generation: Uyen. Despite the ongoing civil and then American war symbolized by the Tết Offensive's uproar, Uyen and her sweetheart, Hai, decide to get married. Following Saigon's fall, My Anh, Quan, Uyen, Hai, and the newlywed's new child try to escape Vietnam by boat. The boat, however, only has room for three adults and the child, so Quan stays behind in hopes of catching the next one—only to be detained at a "reeducation" camp for the rest of his life. Quan's former work for the U.S. secret service, however, enables his family to eventually leave the refugee camp for America.

Act III, "Being American," takes us to the contemporary period in the United States. Uyen and Hai's children, Sara and David, form the "typical Vietnamese family." A dinner conversation breaks out into a contemporary fashion show and then a hip-hop dance performance, the first cued by David's expressed desire to be a fashion designer and the second by Sara's watching MTV as she contemplates marriage even though she will just have finished high school. As mother and daughter disagree, we see that the "typical" family involves lack of understanding between the generations. Sara begins to learn that she has taken for granted the powerful history that her mother, Uyen, and her grandmother, My Anh, experienced during their lives. Following a birthday celebration for the beloved grandfather, Quan, My Anh offers Sara the book that My Anh's own mother had given her in Vietnam. The play ends with Sara reading the book aloud: "Once there was this beautiful girl from the countryside who came to a big city to live and learn. She carried with her no money or riches, only the hopes of her dreams and the promises of her memories."

The Performativity of Performance

There is a notable difference between the performativity of the curriculum, on the one hand, and the performativity of Culture Night and other creative performances set in traditionally staged contexts, on the other. The curriculum asks readers to participate in the performative dimension of the text by completing homework, answering questions, and giving testimony to personal experiences that fit the curricular paradigm. In this sense, the most immediate audience—here, students—is scripted into the performative text, becoming performers themselves by writing and speaking Vietnamese American and American cultural memories. By contrast, the Culture Night performance does not overtly script the audience into the performative act, and we therefore cannot predict the audience's response. A modernist audience may read the performance as a theatrical representation of a story, a representation based on the sharp division between theater and social reality, while a postmodernist audience, if assuming that stories constitute our worlds, may read the performance as another constitution of our constructed realities and engage accordingly. *What Dreams May Come* was a performative that constitutes and reconstitutes Vietnamese and Vietnamese American cultural memories and identity—but, without public reviews available, it is impossible to say whether that performative was felicitously received or even received as a performative among a general anonymous audience.

Regardless of this difference between the curriculum and Culture Night, we might still say that both are performative. Felicity is a goal of performatives, *not* a prior necessary condition. Even if the Culture Night audience's response is largely unknown, what makes the student production performative is that it constructs what culture *is* on this Culture Night. Vietnamese and Vietnamese American culture, in this performance, is based on intergenerational, familial relationships and experiences. VSA's stated purpose in producing Culture Night clarifies the performance's performative purpose: to reconstruct cultural memory and thereby foster solidarity. A letter written from VSA students to local Vietnamese small-business owners, which requested financial support for the 2002 production of Culture Night, attests to the performative nature of Culture Night. Given to me by Lisa, then a second-year student belonging to both VAC and VSA, the letter introduced Culture Night in the following way: "The purpose of the Culture Night is to preserve yesterday's traditions and to incorporate a modern perspective of the evolving Vietnamese American culture through performances such as dances, skits, fashion shows, vocal performances, and live instrumental recitals. The Vietnamese Student Association aims at educating the community across generation lines through building a foundation where parents can understand the modern Vietnamese American culture and children can discover the awesome history of their parents." This letter from VSA students invited community members to commit to strengthening relationships with the younger generation. The letter mirrors Culture Night's larger purpose: to rewrite social relationships that extend beyond the performance's story. The performance and texts surrounding the performance, like the letter, were thus instrumental to bridging generational ruptures caused by diaspora, loss of language, and a perceived loss of heritage.

In the program's foreword William and his coproducer (the 2001–2002 VSA president) wrote another invitation from VSA to the audience,

> The Vietnamese Student Association . . . would like to extend our warmest welcome to you, our honored guests. "What Dreams May Come" is an effort to capture the Vietnamese American interpretation of the struggles and victories of our parents, grandparents, and ancestors. Through this unique collaboration of drama, dance, and music, we address pervasive themes of history such as war, separation, and hope. We would like to thank you, our sponsors, our distinguished faculty, our family, and our friends, for your support throughout the period of preparation for the show and for your presence here tonight. We would also like to apologize in advance for any material that you may find offensive in tonight's show. Please understand that we are students [still] learn-

ing to [mediate] between our two cultures and are subject to misinterpreta-
tions. Now, we present to you "What Dreams May Come."

In depicting the performance as a collaboration "through" which students "mediate between our two cultures," students suggested that the
performance would be instrumental in strengthening social relationships. Faculty, family, peers, and other sponsors (indicated by the writers' thank-yous) evidence how the writers and the audience identified
with a larger Vietnamese American community and encouraged social
bonds beyond that evening's events.

William spoke insightfully about the performative nature of Culture Night when commenting on audiences who might have objected to
Act III's contemporary fashion show as not Vietnamese or even Vietnamese American. He explained: "But, *but* if Vietnamese women are
in it, then it's Vietnamese. Just like, you know, if like they say, um, like,
'Vietnamese people don't do this.' Well, if I'm doing it, it's Vietnamese.
Anything we do, it's basically, it's Vietnamese culture. Anything that's
said, anything you *write*, it's a Vietnamese writer. You know?" Applying this statement to other elements of Culture Night, we might say that
the Vietnamese American actors' acting, the writer's script, and the
dancers' and singers' performances all constitute Vietnamese culture.
Although the Culture Night play is fictional and the medley of dance,
song, and fashion shows was set in a theatrical backdrop, William's
statement suggests that the performance is still a construction of our
reality, of what Vietnamese and Vietnamese American culture is. The
Vietnamese American writers and producers, the Vietnamese American performers, and the social context of a Vietnamese and Vietnamese
American Culture Night set the stage for constructing what culture is,
specifically by constructing memory.

Re-Performing Vietnamese and Vietnamese American Women

William's perspective leads us finally to the ways that his play *What
Dreams May Come* re-presents Vietnamese and Vietnamese American cultures. When I asked William what he hoped to convey through
his script, he responded: "My whole point was to portray strong Vietnamese women. Throughout the ages. They've always been strong. It's
not only that they've been strong just now. That they've been strong
in my great-grandmother's age, my grandmother's, my mom's, and
now present-day. So, I wanted to portray that." Culture Night, then,
is a reconstitution of a Vietnamese and Vietnamese American culture memory where women are foundational. The performance steps
into a potentially democratizing moment, disrupting prior repeated

identifications of Vietnamese and Vietnamese American women with prostitutes and helpless victims. William asserted that even in *Green Dragon*, a 2002 film sympathetic to Vietnamese experiences in a 1975 U.S. refugee camp, he could locate the female characters of "sad, careless mother" and "whore." As we follow the performance of William's play *What Dreams May Come*, we find an emphasis on grandmother-mother-daughter relationships that position strong Vietnamese and Vietnamese American women at the center of history and culture.

What Dreams May Come, I believe, achieves William's goal of representing strong Vietnamese and Vietnamese American women characters. The progression of the three acts layers the experiences of grandmother, mother, and daughter. The following outline lists the play's acts and scenes, interspersed by dance performances, vocal performances, and fashion shows:

ACT I: WHAT DREAMS MAY COME
  Scene 1: 1925 The Birth of New Hopes and Dreams
  Scene 2: Life Changing Decisions
  Scene 3: Better Life in Hanoi
  Solo Performance, "Khong Gia Dinh"
  Scene 4: Quest of the Unlikely Suitors
  Traditional Fashion Show
  Scene 5: Falling for the Busboy
  Solo Performance, "I Can Love You Like That"
  Scene 6: The Truth of Love Revealed

ACT II: THE JOURNEY TOGETHER
  Scene 1: The Apartment of Secret and Lies
  Solo Performance, "Khung Troi Ngay Xua"
  Scene 2: The Migration to Saigon
  Traditional Dance
  Scene 3: Witnesses of the Tet Offensive
  Duet Performance, "Bai Hat Xuan Cho Em"
  Scene 4: Marriage at the Worst of Years
  Scene 5: The Promise Given
  Vocal & Instrumental
  Scene 6: Days in the Refugee Camp
  Scene 7: Ticket to America

ACT III: BEING AMERICAN
  Scene 1: Typical Vietnamese Family
  Modern Fashion Show
  Scene 2: MTV & More . . .
  Modern Dance

With each successive representation of My Anh in the three acts, we see her anew: first as a daughter, sister, and wife; then as a mother; and finally as a grandmother. The representations, therefore, are both culminations and revisions of her former selves. William's grandmother-mother-daughter theme is potentially powerful—in fact, echoing several influential Asian American writers' attention to familial relationships.

In *In Her Mother's House,* scholar Wendy Ho claims that making mother-daughter relationships central in Chinese American literature has worked to assert agency over those social and political forces that have appropriated the telling of their experiences. Ho explains: "The mother-daughter stories indicate a more nuanced and complex understanding of a social-political imaginary that has valuable implications for rethinking notions of identity and sociality. The hard work of talking to each other, for example, can lead toward more compassionate understandings of our differences as well as similarities as women" (238). In *What Dreams May Come,* by talking to her grandmother, My Anh, Sara is able to rethink her own identity. She needs to explore the representations of her grandmother and mother to get past intergenerational misunderstandings. This attention to grandmother-mother-daughter relationships is not based on a naïve sense of womanly camaraderie. Rather, the "hard work of talking to each other" leads to conversations about each woman's specific social and historical experiences. In addition to experiencing political turbulence of colonialism and war, the three generations of women also confront patriarchy, colonialism, classism, and racism. These threads knit together to form cultural memories with women's relationships at their center.

Text becomes a vehicle for accessing these multistoried lives that make up cultural memories. The book that My Anh passes on to Sara holds out the "promises of her memories," but the book itself, taken from the past, *is* the memory being passed on to the next generation. Sara's reading the book enables her (and the audience) to return to the cultural memories of her grandmother's generation but also to reenvision the hope that those memories carry, "what dreams may come." The Culture Night performance of *What Dreams May Come* also becomes a textual vehicle for the *audience* to access intergenerational cultural memories.

Just as the story is instrumental in centralizing female characters, the interspersed dance, song, and fashion show place female performers, choreographers, and costume designers center stage. Christine, an active VAC member who danced in the contemporary hip-hop performance, and William each told me how impressive it was that the contemporary fashion show featured clothes designed and made by a female VSA student. Although William was impressed by the student-produced fashion show, he expressed dissatisfaction with having to integrate seemingly disparate performances (like the contemporary fashion show) into the play, when they had little to do with the storyline. Because Culture Night is always a collaborative production and traditionally includes fashion shows, William needed to include the fashion shows even if they did not quite fit into the play's storyline. From my perspective, these insertions of musical performances or fashion shows did seem disjointed, although the varied performances created a thought-provoking ensemble. My sense that the fashion show and several other performances did not connect to the play's storyline, interestingly, led me to see these performances as more immediate than the play.

This immediacy showcased the students as live performers more than as fictional characters. With the backdrop of strong women in the play, this immediacy further placed the spotlight on Vietnamese American women. The Culture Night performance of the play *What Dreams May Come* thus not only represents Vietnamese and Vietnamese American women characters in a fictional realm but also presents Vietnamese American actors, dancers, choreographers, singers, fashion designers, and models at the event. Both fictional characters and live performers merge to constitute Vietnamese and Vietnamese American cultures. As performance studies scholar Marvin Carlson has cautioned, however, we need to understand performatives as enacting both subversion and complicity. Despite William's efforts to present and re-present strong Vietnamese and Vietnamese American women, a mishap at the contemporary fashion show, in which one model's top slipped to her waist, called attention to the persistent objectification of women. William described feedback that VSA received about this specific incident at Culture Night: "Well, if you go on the website [name omitted], you'll see that most of the positive compliments are from males who said, 'The fashion show was just kickass.' 'Let's, let's see that girl's top drop one more time.' Or, 'The girls were hot.' Or like stuff like that." These responses, too, become scripted into the "culture" that Culture Night constitutes. Such performances are neither universal nor idealistic presentations of Vietnamese and Vietnamese American culture but, like the Vietnamese American curriculum, they enter into the intertextual web of subversion and complicity that continue to revise the signifier of "Vietnamese American." Solidarity among the producers, the performers, and the audience was based on the shared understanding of Vietnamese and Vietnamese American culture that this Culture Night performed. Most immediately, this intertextual web included the performance itself, the Culture Night program, the VSA letter soliciting community support for the performance, feedback about the performance, and finally the countless, varied talk and writing in the weeks before and after Culture Night. The performance became a basis for writers, performers, and community members to identify with the intergenerational cultural memory depicted in Culture Night and therefore to identify with one another.

"You Make Whatever America Is": Performance Art and Textual Art

Now I turn to performance art ("Un-Gender-Eyes" and "Speak American Damn It!") and textual art ("I LOVE YOUR ACCENT" and "I WANT A THICKER ACCENT") to elucidate the dialogue and mutual recognition that may grow out of engagement between performers and audience. These performance and textual art pieces subvert audience expectations, and in those moments opened up by subversive moves, the performers challenge the audience toward mutual understanding and new identifications.

Mutual Performativity in "Un-Gender-Eyes"

In June, VAC student Duc invited me to a student production that had grown out of his performance art course. Duc and Mai, also a VAC student performed in the show: Mai performing "Un-Gender-Eyes" and, later, Duc, Mai, and a second student performing "Speak American Damn It!" In "Un-Gender-Eyes," Mai stands center-stage and two students hold a flat sheet vertically in front of her body. She walks around to the front of the sheet and, with blunt strokes of a black marker, outlines the shape of her body. She then takes a knife and slashes parts of the sheet that represent body parts: her mouth, her genitalia. In a climactic gesture, she puts the sheet back on her body, walks off the stage toward the audience, takes the sheet off, and places it on a man in the audience.

While her performance includes no spoken or written words except for the title "Un-Gender-Eyes," the performance starkly illustrates the solidarity that can result or can be thwarted by interaction. At stake in this interaction are issues of performer-audience agency and mutuality, alluded to in Mai's interview account of her performance:

> And then the . . . piece . . . pertained to sexual violence. And what I wanted to do was show how, like, society or patriarchy has placed the blame on the victim. The shame lies with the person that the violence has been placed upon, done to. And, um, what happens is, like, putting on the sheet, you step into or you become the victim yourself. And then the shame, At the end I took off the shame, right? I wanted to give it to someone. And I wanted to give it to a male person in the audience. So part of it too, like, it's not just a women's issue, but it's a societal issue. And that men need to understand and connect and really empathize. Like put on the sheet over themselves. Feel the shame and feel what the women would feel if they were raped or beaten.

Mai takes what is sadly a commonplace in our culture (sexual violence and victimized women)—an image that has become normalized through repetition. This performance is a repetition of the commonplace but with variation, where Mai confers the status of victim from an individual woman over to a male audience member. Through her assertion of performative agency, Mai creates an imperative for mutuality. By placing the sheet, or the shame, on a man in the audience, she invites the audience, specifically this man, to identify with the victim. He is asked to move beyond the role of sympathetic spectator and to participate, to actively identify with the victim. No longer a voyeur, the audience member must take responsibility for his new understanding.

As an invitation, Mai's performance caused the man and onlookers like me to question our role in the performance, to wonder what the sheet symbolized, and to consider whether the man should accept it. More overtly performative than the Culture Night production, "Un-Gender-Eyes" scripts the audience into the performance. That is to say, the meaning of the performance erupts from the performatives that Mai and the audience each issue or fail to issue. In fact, the title of the performance, "Un-Gender-Eyes," might be read as a performative utterance. Could the title be read as an imperative, a commanding invitation to deconstruct gender? "Ungender, Eyes!" Or perhaps, with a play on sound, Mai's rhetorical gesture is the action itself: the process of "ungenderizing" the audience. In both cases the audience can "ungender" by crossing gender constructions to empathize and take action against sexual violence.

To "ungenderize," the audience requires courage because its response is wholly unpredictable. Mai described the audience member's reaction at this show: "I don't know, he just took it. It was very interesting. He accepted it, but I guess it's also because it's a performance, like what is he going to do? I'm sure he was shocked. He's like, 'Why me?,' right? When I did it the first time in class, I chose a person in class. And when I gave him the shame, he didn't want to take it. He's like, 'Why, why me?' He thought that I was placing blame on him, like he was the perpetrator." This keen observation hones in on the risks in generating new vocabularies, new meanings. As speakers and writers attempt to buck convention and to create new vocabularies that can heighten solidarity, they can also risk alienating the audience. The risk can often result in a defensive measure, a sense that "This is not mine" or "Why me?" This male student's response, interestingly, might be read as a complete identification with the victim: "Why me?" However, without becoming aware of the doubleness of performance art, where he might enact a constructed role and also reflect on that role, this audience member could become immobilized by the performance. Mai assessed this student's response well: "I *think* men avoid that because they're afraid they're going to be looked at as the perpetrator, you know. As the enemy. But that's not the issue." The issue, rather, is to create an ability to empathize and build solidarity that is not only nominal but that places all parties at risk and makes all parties vulnerable to the community. In "Un-Gender-Eyes," involvement is risky. Mai thus compels us to consider how performative agency and mutuality come together to produce new meaning as risky as that production might be.

Mutuality Reinforced in "Speak American Damn It!"

A second performance in this student production also strives toward a sense of mutuality—this time, making the audience's tendency toward self-centeredness even more alarmingly apparent. Mai, Duc, and another classmate performed "Speak American Damn It!" Before this performance, another performer was crushing aluminum cans on the stage. As the performer clears the cans off the stage, the audience hears a loud conversation and boisterous laughter from three performers. The "beginning" of the piece is unclear. Mai, Duc, and a third student are engaged in a lively and colorful conversation for about ten minutes: talking trash, joking about sex, cursing Ho Chi Minh—but completely in Vietnamese. Although the audience is ethnically and racially diverse, most people probably could not understand the language. The conversation ends as it begins, with no clear boundaries.

Later, when asked to describe the performance, Mai said:

That was just, like, some random conversation that we, um, kind of did in the audience, and we spoke in Vietnamese. And the point of that is that like, whenever, like in the United States, you're always forced to speak English. Like when you, when you arrived here as refugees or immigrants, whatever, like you immediately are forced to speak English and you're immersed into this culture. And, even when you go outside of the country, you expect other people to speak English, or Americans expect other people to speak English, right? So that was kind of like a play on that. And we used "American" because people always referred and have associated English as the American language, and we wanted to emphasize that English is not American. That American can be anything. Like, speaking American or whatever. Because America is, like, multicultural, speaking Vietnamese is speaking "American," quote unquote, right? So. And also we wanted to create a level of, like, discomfort for people in the room that did not speak Vietnamese and who could not understand.

Duc described the performance similarly: "I describe it as exhilarating because you know what? That threat always exists in America of not speaking English and knowing that people around you don't understand you because they will be very defensive towards that. It felt exhilarating because although we may or may not be talking about them, the listeners may not understand us. They feel very threatened. They do. And, and they should feel comfortable. We want to create that." Once again, agency and mutuality figure as important to this performance. The students perform the "threat" or "discomfort" that people often feel when hearing a language that they don't understand, often a language other than English. The Vietnamese-only conversation creates an in-group and an out-group, highlighting the cultural capital that language can carry. The issue of how monolingualism or multilingualism might create in- and out-groups, in effect, calls attention to how multilingualism could be (but is often not) perceived as invitational.

Interestingly, Duc reinscribed the "threat" with a *dual* meaning during his interview account of the performance. In addition to the audience's feelings of discomfort, he cited the multilingual speakers as being threatened by those who only speak English: "That threat always exists in American of not speaking English and knowing that people around you don't understand you." Duc's statement implies that the ones threatened, in fact, are the people not speaking English while in an English-only environment. They are threatened by English-only speakers who are prejudiced against their multilingualism. Having reinscribed the "threat" with new meaning, the performers create a sense of mutual participation with the audience by sitting in the audience. While they re-create the discomfort, there is also something welcoming in the lively, boisterous laughter. As Duc explained, "they should feel comfortable" because the performers try to create that comfort. The title of the piece "Speak American Damn It!" embodies both the discomfort and the desire for comfort. We might read it as an imperative delivered by those who feel threatened by non-English language. Or if we understand "American" to take on new meaning, we might hear "Speak American Damn It!" as a reinscription of the meaning of "American." In Duc's words: "There's no such thing as American. You make whatever America is. You create your own America."

Finally, as we read the performance more closely, we might locate yet one more nuance. Those who later learn the subject matter of the conversation soon realize that there is a layer of gender politics in this performance. The talk is raunchy and abrasive, as Mai later explained:

> Like, it's very raw. Basically talking about sex, or like who has the bigger penis. And like, it was just like a random, macho-istic, masculine, like, atmosphere where I guess, I guess I'm supposed to represent the girl who's, I guess there's a gender kind of thing in it, but that's another level. Who's trying to fit into this conversation where they're talking about, "Who has the bigger penis?" "Let me see yours." "Do you want to suck my dick?" Whatever, whatever.

Even in our interview Mai was hesitant to repeat the "raw" language of the performance, toning down the impact of the sexual language and not mentioning how the performers curse and laugh about cursing Ho Chi Minh. Although neither Mai nor Duc commented much on the gender issues here (and this is surprising, since both actively reject conventional constructions of gender), Mai's role in the conversation as a woman among two men talking about penises impacts the interaction among performers and audience. One issue at stake in the conversation was how the woman of the group rhetorically makes a space for herself in the conversation. Such a realization highlights the degree to which our reaction as audience members is self-centered. While we may be squirming in our seats, thinking about how we feel threatened by a language we don't understand, we miss how Mai must navigate this masculine space. What we learn is that the talk is not only about *individuals* but about the *mutual* construction of meaning, a continual effort to invite another in and to identify with that other.

Ellipses in Textual Art

A third artist and also a VAC student, Son, created textual art that engenders the kind of mutuality raised by the two works of performance art, a mutuality where performer and audience step into a newly formed space created by the performative text. Notably, Son's textual art goes beyond the bounds of a staged production. While the two performance art pieces that we have explored undoubtedly took great rhetorical risks to heighten audience involvement, we should keep in mind that these were performed in the context of a show where the audience was probably more amenable to experimentation and risk-taking. Rather than using confrontational strategies, Son's textual art draws on a discursive strategy that would perhaps appeal to a wider audience: ellipses. Linguist Deborah Tannen has described an ellipsis as a strategy for involvement and elaborates that "by requiring the listener or reader to fill in unstated meaning, indirectness [and ellipsis and silence] contribute to a sense of involvement through mutual participation in sensemaking" (23). For Tannen, such ellipsis can invoke shared understanding among speakers. In the terms used in this project, we might describe an ellipsis as an invitation, an opening for an audience to enter the conversation initiated by the inviter.

In June, Son invited me to an exhibition of senior art majors' final projects. An art major himself, Son guided me through his friends' works and explained how he enjoyed art that invoked response or made social commentary. Having his portfolio on hand, Son showed me an example. He had created two 8 ½ x 11-inch sheets that stated "I LOVE YOUR ACCENT" and "I WANT A THICKER ACCENT." Explaining that people often say that they find French and British accents attractive, he questioned why English spoken with Asian accents is not perceived similarly. He posted countless flyers around campus, primarily around the fine arts corner of campus.

Needless to say, the response to them was curiosity and discussion. The unknown author, the ambiguity of the message, and the minimal context around the flyers contributed to an invitational ellipses, openings in which others could offer their perspectives. Son explained that he would overhear people passing by the flyers question their meaning. In doing so, these passersby responded to the invitation and, joining the dialogue that Son had created, he identified with their viewpoints and shared his own. The innovative flyers offered a revision to the viewers' understanding of English spoken with Asian accents. Through dialogue and inquiry, the speakers jointly constructed a more textured perspective on language. Son created an opportunity for people to talk about their assumptions about accents, language, and respect.

These works of textual art did not appeal to as many people as the curriculum and Culture Night performances had. However, like Duc and Mai's performance art, Son's texts invited dialogue between the writer and his audience and encouraged mutual recognition among linguistically diverse students. Dialogue inspired by the students' works (both performance and textual art) thereby rhetorically performed a coming together of people and worldviews.

I LOVE YOUR ACCENT

I WANT A THICKER ACCENT

When the OCAPICA curriculum committee generously gave me a copy of *Vietnamese Americans: Lessons in American History* in April 2002, I was delighted—not only because I thought that this curriculum was valuable for the local Vietnamese community but also because I had grown up in Los Angeles and later Orange County and thus identified with Vietnamese American students' potential excitement about the curriculum's contents. That evening, I shared the curriculum with two of my childhood friends, both Vietnamese American and both still living in Orange County. We stopped to look at a timeline of the major waves of immigration to the United States and again to read reprinted newspaper articles about hate crimes and political protests. Identifying the points representing our own families' immigration and talking about our memories of the news headlines, there was an uncanny sense of connection.

It was then—upon reflection about the ways that the curriculum could instill in youth a shared knowledge about Vietnamese American history and upon reflection about what my friends and I shared in a more local interaction—that I came to see memory and performative texts, specifically as they take shape in language, literacy, and rhetoric, as powerful and hopeful. In the history of U.S. education, we find that speaking and writing positions are delimited by legacies of racial discrimination. In composing and performing public texts that re-perform our identities, recollect cultural memories, and rearticulate Asian American subject positions, Asian American activists call on educators to scrutinize more deeply the ways in which legacies of racism continue to haunt speakers and writers.

Worth noting is Asian American studies scholar Lisa Lowe's caution: "Alternative cultural forms and practices do not offer havens of resolution but are often eloquent descriptions of the ways in which the law, labor exploitation, racialization, and gendering work to prohibit alternatives. Some cultural forms succeed in making it possible to live and inhabit alternatives in the encounter with those prohibitions; some permit us to imagine what we have still yet to live" (x). These performances foster precisely this critical remembering and imagining. We may cautiously renew our hope that language, literacy, and rhetorical education can once more help us promote an approach to composition that allows us, as feminist theorist Judith Butler suggests, to "open new contexts" and "speak in ways that have never yet been legitimated" (*Excitable Speech* 41).

Afterword

Writing against Racial Injury, Writing to Remember

This book reflects my efforts to engage in memory work. Throughout these pages I have recollected the disquieting interplay of race, language, and literacy in American education in the post–civil rights era—in particular, I have studied Asian American student activists in California who contested constraints on their speaking positions, their language and literacy education, and their rhetorical engagement in seemingly postracial discourses. And I have invited readers to bear witness to sites of Asian American activism: the growth of Asian American student organizations and self-sponsored writing; the ways language served as thinly veiled tropes for race in the influential *Lau v. Nichols*; the inheritance of a rhetoric of injury, which paradoxically encouraged struggles for racial justice but also frustrated student discourse; and alternative rhetorical strategies that rearticulate Asian American racial identity.

Building on Lisa Lowe's oft-cited text *Immigrant Acts*, I argue that this book illustrates what she has called alternative sites of cultural production. "Asian American culture," Lowe writes, "'re-members' the past in and through the fragmentation, loss, and dispersal that constitutes that past" (29). Indeed, these fragments of Asian American educational history depict a troubling repetition of racial projects that continue to differentiate Asian American speaking and writing subjects as perpetual foreigners and thus absent from the American imaginary; such racial projects, in turn, reflect back on the normative American speaking and writing subject and the need to interrogate the ways in which this norm has been defined. At the same time, these fragments present hopeful ways for educators, researchers, and practitioners of language, literacy, and rhetoric to engage with our racial legacy and to rearticulate Asian American speaking and writing positions.

It's well documented that people of Asian heritage have been racially othered in the United States at least since the nineteenth century and likely earlier: Asian Americans as foreigners, yellow peril, threat to "native" laborers, feminized men, hypersexualized women, model minorities, and more. As Michael Omi and Howard Winant have argued, "racial formation is a process of historically situated *projects* in which human bodies and social structures are represented and organized." And "a racial formation," their explanation continues, "is simultaneously an interpretation, representation, or explanation of racial dynamics, or an effort to reorganize and redistribute resources along particular racial lines" (55–56). While we have a limited view into the history of Asian American education in the United States, sadly what we glimpse is not *education*. Rather, this is a history of *racial projects* that differentiated Asian Americans: restrictions from public schools, suspicion of heritage language schools, segregation based on linguistic backgrounds, denial of English language instruction after inclusion, and denial of a curriculum that reflects Asian American experiences and concerns.

Moreover, each fragment, each racial project cannot be read in isolation, divorced from the historical moment and social context. Rather, I *re-collect* these racial projects into one book in an attempt to illustrate the fact that—despite the absence of archives and histories of Asian Americans speaking and writing in the United States in the past century and a half—the sparse records point to racial projects that collect, pile up, and thus gain performative force. Given institutional authority and repetition of racial projects for more than a century, the racial formation of Asian Americans has been cemented into the American imaginary. For this reason, Asian American language, literacy, and rhetorical education must be interpreted against the backdrop of racial legacies in the United States.

Such memory work, in fact, has helped me re-collect and make sense of experiences that I have had in my own professional life. These are experiences that seemed isolated, but in hindsight I now see the ways in which they illustrate the ways in which racial formation of Asian

Americans have implications for one's language and literacy education and practices. Consider these few memories of mine:

> When I was in my early twenties, I tutored the two sons of a wealthy family from Japan (ethnically Korean, the father would insist) because the public school in this affluent neighborhood had limited English language support for these boys and their French classmate with nonmainstream needs.

> When I worked part-time for the Boy and Girl Scout Service's Learning for Life program, I gave community-building lessons to Vietnamese-track, Spanish-track, and "mainstream" classes in one of Oakland's inner-city schools. One day, a few third-grade girls in the Vietnamese track held my hands tightly and smiled. I *must* be their teacher's sister, they said; that was the only way that they could explain the existence of *two* Vietnamese American teachers.

> When I began teaching composition, I taught basic writing to mostly first-generation college students and mostly racial minority and/or first-generation immigrant students. A Chinese American student asked why he was originally placed in the ESL basic writing track when he only spoke English. He grew up in a neighborhood in Oakland where AAVE [African American Vernacular English] was the dominant dialect.

> Teaching writing at research universities, I have had the occasional Asian American students confide to me: I am not a good writer. I am not a good writer. *We* [Asians, Asian Americans] are not good writers. You [the Asian American writing teacher] must be an exception.

> At one of the annual Conferences on College Composition and Communication, a distinguished scholar in the field said he had a first-generation immigrant graduate student who identified with her country of origin in Southeast Asia. Does she need to know about Asian American history even if she doesn't identify as Asian American? Yes, I said.

Without understanding the racial legacies that inform how Asian Americans are traditionally positioned in relation to language, literacy, and rhetoric, it would be easy to read these memories in terms of language deficiencies, personalities, and low self-esteem. It is much harder but more informative to discern how racial legacies linger and how Asian Americans might redefine the conversation.

But Asian American sites of cultural production *do* have the potential to generate critique as well as rearticulations, as Lowe has explained: "Asian American culture is the site of more than critical negation of the US nation; it is a site that shifts and marks alternatives to the national terrain by occupying other spaces, imagining different narratives and critical historiographies, and enacting practices that give rise to new forms of subjectivity and new ways of questioning the government of human life by the nation state" (29). Throughout this research project, I have worked to recognize Asian American activists who rearticulate their speaking and writing positions, demand "self-determination," and re-member and re-perform what is Asian American and what is American. It's here, I argue, that we see Asian American rhetoric at work. Even as Asian Americans embody heterogeneity on many levels, what Asian American rhetorics share are the use of linguistic and other symbolic systems to contest Asian American racial formation and to rearticulate the subject positions available to Asian Americans.

Furthermore, because language and literacy have been used to racialize Asian Americans as the foreign or invisible other, Asian American activist rhetoric has been about rearticulating the subject positions not only of Asian American speakers and writers but, more broadly, *American* speakers and writers—and it has been about rearticulating American traditions of language, literacy, and rhetoric. Put another way, rather than define language, literacy, and rhetoric in terms of abstractions like virtue and power, what would it look like if we were to define these concepts in a more grounded, ethnographic way through the multivalent experiences of racial minority and majority speakers and writers? What would it look like if we were to work toward *copia—*full, messy, associative—as we weave together a shared yet divergent fabric of linguistic, literate, and rhetorical traditions? What would it mean to "look to the bottom" in our work as educators and researchers in language, literacy, and rhetoric?

Writing against racial injury, at least for the Asian American activists who've populated this book, has entailed copiously *remembering* of racial legacies and *performing/re-performing* new ways of understanding their roles as speakers and writers, new perspectives on language, literacy, and rhetoric. Asian American rearticulations of racialized subject positions have been carried out through activism for language minorities (with community activists, with/against school administrators, in courts), literacy acts (extracurricular publications, new curricula, creative works), and rhetorical means (cultural memory, performativity). I argue that such cultural production truly matters, as Morris Young has urged as well: "As America enters the twenty-first century and many institutions, including our educational institutions, move to address issues of diversity and the intellectual value of examining our many American cultures, there is a need for vigilance and action in making sure that our minor narratives do not remain between the drafts of the American Story" (*Minor Re/Visions* 192). Indeed, as the ethnographic case study of Vietnamese American Coalition (VAC) student discourse illustrates, it is memory and performance that allows

Asian American activists in the twenty-first century to not only write against racial injury but also to write against the *discourses of racial injury* that too often govern racial accountability in what is seen as a postracial moment.

As educators and researchers of language, literacy, and rhetoric, we too must learn how to engage race and work toward racial accountability while avoiding what Carl Gutiérrez-Jones has called the "logic of moral equivalence" where we can only relate as injurer or injured. While it is not the goal of this book to delineate specific practices for researchers or teachers, and while it would not make sense to appropriate wholesale rhetorical strategies illustrated by Asian Americans in this book who have their own purposes and contexts, I would like to close with a gesture toward such questions. *Re-membering* racial legacies and *performing/re-performing* new perspectives on racial minority people and our relationship to language, literacy, and rhetoric are important to the inquiry that we practice as researchers as well as the inquiry that we work to foster as teachers.

As teachers, we can ask students to engage in memory work to collaboratively question how racial legacies have informed American traditions of language, literacy, and rhetoric. We can ask students to place their own heritage languages, literacy histories, and ethnic rhetorical traditions alongside critical historiographies on language, literacy, and rhetoric. And we can ask students to recognize the ways in which, as Young has suggested, they might have minor narratives to contribute to the "American Story." And as researchers, we can engage in such inquiry ourselves by juxtaposing ethnography with historiography; drawing connections among ethnic studies, critical race theory, literacy studies, and rhetorical theories and histories; and re-collecting and reading ethnic minority rhetorics in the context of racial formation. In essence, what these researcher and teacher lines of inquiry share is a deep curiosity about the ways in which racial formation clings onto language, literacy, and rhetorical education and practices and a desire to engage in a rhetoric that recalls these racial legacies and works toward racial accountability.

Works Cited

Affeldt, John T. "Report on Strand B: Legal/Legislative Policy." Proceedings of the Symposium *Revisiting the* Lau *Decision: 20 Years After.* Ed. Sau-Lim Tsang. 3–4 Nov. 1994. 18–23. ARC Associates. Web. 15 Dec. 2008.

Altbach, Philip, and Robert Cohen. "American Student Activism: The Post-Sixties Transformation." *Journal of Higher Education* 61.1 (1990). 32–49. JSTOR. Web. 20 Feb. 2008.

Anzaldúa, Gloria. *Borderlands/La Frontera: The New Mestiza.* San Francisco: Spinsters/Aunt Lute Books, 1987. Print.

Austin, J. L. *How to Do Things with Words.* Cambridge, MA: Harvard UP, 1962. Print.

Baker, Colin. *Foundations of Bilingual Education and Bilingualism.* 5th ed. Tonawanda, NY: Multilingual Matters, 2011. Print.

Ball, Arnetha, and Ted Lardner. "Dispositions toward Language: Teacher Constructs of Knowledge and the Ann Arbor Black English Case." *College Composition and Communication* 48.4 (1997): 469–85. JSTOR. Web. 13 Dec. 2006.

Barnett, Timothy. "Reading 'Whiteness' in English Studies." *College English* 63.1 (2000): 9–37. Print.

Baron, Dennis E. *The English-Only Question: An Official Language for Americans?* New Haven: Yale UP, 1990. Print.

Baron, Dennis E. "Federal English." *Language Loyalties*. Ed. James Crawford. Chicago: U of Chicago P, 1992. 36–40. Print.

Beevi, Mariam, James C. Lam, and Michael Matsuda. "Transforming the Curriculum: Incorporating the Vietnamese American Experience into K–12 Education." *Amerasia Journal* 29.1 (2003): 165–78. Print.

Bell, Derrick A., Jr. "Serving Two Masters: Integration Ideals and Client Interests in School Desegregation Litigation." 1976. *Critical Race Theory: The Key Writings That Informed the Movement*. Eds. Kimberlé Crenshaw, Neil Gotanda, Gary Peller, and Kendall Thomas. New York: The New Press, 1995. 5–19. Print.

Bonilla-Silva, Eduardo. *Racism without Racists: Color-Blind Racism and the Persistence of Racial Inequality in the United States*. 2nd ed. Lanham, MD: Rowman & Littlefield Publishers, 2006. Print.

Boylan, Anne. *Sunday School: The Formation of an American Institution, 1790–1880*. New Haven: Yale UP, 1988. Print.

Brandt, Deborah. "Accumulating Literacy: Writing and Learning to Write in the Twentieth Century." *College English* 67.6 (1995): 649–68. JSTOR. Web. 7 Aug. 2008.

Brandt, Deborah. *Literacy in American Lives*. Cambridge: Cambridge UP, 2001. Print.

Butler, Judith. *Bodies That Matter: On the Discursive Limits of "Sex."* New York and London: Routledge, 1993. Print.

Butler, Judith. *Excitable Speech: The Politics of Performativity*. New York and London: Routledge, 1997. Print.

Canagarajah, A. Suresh. "The Place of World Englishes in Composition: Pluralization Continued." *College Composition and Communication* 57.4 (2006): 586–619. Print.

Carlson, Marvin. *Performance: A Critical Introduction*. London and New York: Routledge, 1996. Print.

Carruthers, Mary. *The Book of Memory: A Study of Memory in Medieval Culture*. Cambridge: Cambridge UP, 1990. Print.

Chan, Sucheng. *Asian Americans: An Interpretive History*. Boston: Twayne, 1991. Print.

Chandrasekaran, Rajiv. "In Vietnam, McCain Finds Unlikely Allies; Despite Ex-POW's Slur, Many Former Foes Support Candidacy." *Washington Post*, 28 Feb. 2000, A9. LexisNexis Academic. Web. 10 Aug. 2006.

"City College Faculty Endorses Black Studies and Recruiting of the Poor." *New York Times*, 15 May 1969. ProQuest Historical Newspapers. Web. 12 Dec. 2007.

Climo, Jacob J., and Maria G. Catell. "Meaning in Social Memory and History: Anthropological Perspectives." *Social Memory and History: Anthropological Perspectives*. Eds. Jacob J. Climo and Maria G. Catell. Walnut Creek, CA: Altamira P, 2002. Print.

Cornelius, Janet Duitsman. *When I Can Read My Title Clear: Literacy, Slavery, and Religion in the Antebellum South*. Columbia: U of South Carolina P, 1991. Print.

Crawford, James, ed. *Language Loyalties: A Sourcebook on the Official English Controversy*. Chicago: U of Chicago P, 1992. Print.

Crowley, Sharon. *The Methodical Memory: Invention in Current-Traditional Rhetoric.* Carbondale: Southern Illinois UP, 1990. Print.

Crowley, Sharon. "Modern Rhetoric and Memory." *Rhetorical Memory and Delivery: Classical Concepts for Contemporary Composition and Communication.* Ed. John Frederick Reynolds. Hillsdale, NJ: Lawrence Erlbaum Associates, 1993. 31–44. Print.

Crowley, Sharon. *Toward a Civil Discourse: Rhetoric and Fundamentalism.* Pittsburgh: U of Pittsburgh P, 2006. Print.

Cushman, Ellen. *The Struggle and the Tools: Oral and Literate Strategies in an Inner City Community.* Albany: State U of New York P, 1998. Print.

Dillard, J.L. *Black English: Its History and Usage in the United States.* New York: Random House, 1972. Print.

"Editorial." *Gidra* 1.7 (Oct. 1969): 4. Print.

"Editorial." *Gidra* 2.4 (April 1970): 4–5. Print.

"Editor's Note." *Gidra* 6.4 (April 1974): 3. Print.

Enoch, Jessica. "Resisting the Script of Indian Education: Zitkala Ša and the Carlisle Indian School." *College English* 65.2 (2002): 117–41. Print.

Euchner, Charlie. "Languages, Law, and San Francisco." *Education Week.* 25 Jan. 1984. Web. 6 Oct. 2014.

Farr, Marcia. "En Los Dos Idiomas." *Literacy across Communities.* Ed. Beverly Moss. Creskill, NJ: Hampton P, 1994. 9-47. Print.

Francoz, Marion Joan. "Habit as Memory Incarnate." *College English* 62.1 (1999): 11–29. Print.

Gándara, Patricia, Rachel Moran, and Eugene Garcia. "Legacy of *Brown: Lau* and Language Policy in the United States." *Review of Research in Education* 28 (2004): 27–46. Print.

Gere, Anne Ruggles. "Kitchen Tables and Rented Rooms: The Extracurriculum of Composition." *College Composition and Communication* 45.1 (1994): 75–92. JSTOR. Web. 6 Aug. 2008.

Gere, Anne Ruggles. *Writing Groups: History, Theory, and Implications.* Carbondale: Southern Illinois UP, 1987. Print.

"Gidra." *Gidra* 1.1 (April 1969): 2. Print.

Gilyard, Keith. "Higher Learning: Composition's Racialized Reflection." *Race, Rhetoric, and Composition.* Ed. Keith Gilyard. Portsmouth, NH: Boynton/Cook, 1999. 44–52. Print.

Gilyard, Keith. *Voices of the Self: A Study of Language Competence.* Detroit: Wayne State UP, 1991. Print.

Gordon, Edward E., and Elaine H. Gordon. *Literacy in America: Historic Journey and Contemporary Solutions.* Westport, CT: Praeger, 2003. Print.

Gossett, Thomas F. *Race: The History of an Idea in America.* New York: Oxford UP, 1997. Print.

Guerra, Juan. *Close to Home: Oral and Literate Practices in a Transnational Mexicano Community.* New York: Teachers College P, 1998. Print.

Gutiérrez-Jones, Carl. *Critical Race Narratives: A Study of Race, Rhetoric, and Injury.* New York: New York UP, 2001. Print.

Halperin, Irving. "Do You Know What's Happening?" *English Journal* 58.7 (1969): 1049–52. Web. 17 Dec. 2007.

Haney López, Ian. *White by Law: The Legal Construction of Race.* 1996. New York: New York UP, 2006. Print.

Havelock, Eric A. *The Muse Learns to Write: Reflections on Orality and Literacy from Antiquity to the Present.* New Haven: Yale UP, 1986. Print.

Hawkins, John. "Politics, Education, and Language Policy: The Case of Japanese Language Schools in Hawaii." *The Asian American Educational Experience: A Sourcebook for Teachers and Students.* Eds. Don T. Nakanishi and Tina Yamano Nishida. New York: Routledge, 1995. 30–41. Print.

Heath, Shirley Brice. *Ways with Words: Language, Life, and Work in Communities and Classrooms.* New York: Cambridge UP, 1983. Print.

Heath, Shirley Brice. "Why No Official Tongue?" 1976. *Language Loyalties.* Ed. James Crawford. Chicago: U of Chicago P, 1992. 20–31. Print.

Hernandez, Greg. "Grisly Account of Ly Killing Believed Penned by Suspect." *Los Angeles Times.* 7 March 1996, A. LexisNexis Academic. Web. 10 Aug. 2006.

Himley, Margaret. "Response to Phillip P. Marzluf, 'Diversity Writing: Natural Languages, Authentic Voices.'" *College Composition and Communication* 58.3 (2007): 449–63. Print.

Ho, Wendy. *In Her Mother's House: The Politics of Asian American Mother-Daughter Writing.* Walnut Creek, CA: Altamira P, 1999.

hooks, bell. *Teaching to Transgress: Education as the Practice of Freedom.* New York: Routledge, 1994. Print.

Hum, Sue. "'Yes, We Eat Dog Back Home': Contrasting Disciplinary Discourse and Praxis on Diversity." *JAC* 19.4 (1999): 569–87. Print.

Hymes, Dell. *Foundations in Sociolinguistics: An Ethnographic Approach.* Philadelphia: U of Pennsylvania P, 1974. Print.

Inkelas, Karen Kurotsuchi. "Does Participation in Ethnic Cocurricular Activities Facilitate a Sense of Ethnic Awareness and Understanding? A Study of Asian Pacific American Undergraduates." *Journal of College Student Development* 45.3 (2004): 285–302. Project Muse. Web. 11 March 2010.

Iwasaki, Bruce. "The Final Venomous Jabberwocky: Feverish Grunts on the Movement and the Word." *Gidra* 6.4 (April 1974): 5. Print.

Kanji. "The Third World: A Response to Oppression." *Gidra* 1.1 (April 1969): 1, 4. Print.

Kates, Susan. "Literacy, Voting Rights, and the Citizenship Schools in the South, 1957–1970." *College Composition & Communication* 57.3 (2006): 479–502. Print.

Keating, AnnLouise. "Interrogating 'Whiteness,' (De)Constructing 'Race.'" *College English* 57.8 (1995): 901–18. JSTOR. Web. 18 Dec. 2006.

Kiang, Peter N. "'We Could Shape It': Organizing for Asian Pacific American Student Empowerment." *Struggling to Be Heard: The Unmet Needs of Asian Pacific Ameri-*

can Children. Eds. Valerie Ooka Pang and Li-Rong Lilly Cheng. Albany: State U of New York P, 1998. 243–64. *NetLibrary*. Web. 1 June 2010.

Kim, Elaine H. *Asian American Literature: An Introduction to the Writings and Their Social Context*. Philadelphia: Temple UP, 1982. Print.

Kubota, Larry. "Yellow Power!" *Gidra* 1.1 (April 1969): 3–4. Print.

Labov, William. *Language in the Inner City: Studies in the Black English Vernacular*. Philadelphia: U of Pennsylvania P, 1972. Print.

Lam, Andrew. "Goodbye, Saigon, Finally." *PBS* POV "Regarding War." 23 Nov. 1996. Web. 22 Mar. 2015.

Lau v. Nichols. 414 U.S. 563 (1974). Westlaw Campus Research. Web. 12 Oct. 2007.

Lau v. Nichols. 483 F.2d 791 (9th Cir. 1973). Westlaw Campus Research. Web. 12 Oct. 2007.

Lawrence, Charles R., III. "The Id, the Ego, and Equal Protection: Reckoning with Unconscious Racism." 1987. *Critical Race Theory: The Key Writings That Informed the Movement*. Eds. Kimberlé Crenshaw, Neil Gotanda, Gary Peller, and Kendall Thomas. New York: New Press, 1995. 235–57. Print.

LeCourt, Donna. *Identity Matters: Schooling the Student Body in Academic Discourse*. Albany: State U of New York, 2004. Print.

Lee, Chang-Rae. *Native Speaker*. New York: Riverhead Books, 1995. Print.

Leung, Constant, Roxy Harris, and Ben Rampton. "The Idealised Native Speaker, Reified Ethnicities, and Classroom Realities." *TESOL Quarterly* 31.3 (1997): 543–60. Print.

Leverenz, Carrie Shively. "Collaboration, Race, and the Rhetoric of Evasion." *JAC* 16.2 (1996): 297–312. Print.

Lopez, Lori. "The Yellow Press: Asian American Radicalism and Conflict in *Gidra*." *Annual Meeting of the International Communication Association*. Marriott, Chicago, IL. 20 May 2009. All Academic. Web. 11 March 2010.

Low, Victor. *The Unimpressible Race: A Century of Educational Struggle by the Chinese in San Francisco*. San Francisco: East/West Publishing, 1982. Print.

Lowe, Lisa. *Immigrant Acts: On Asian American Cultural Politics*. Durham. Duke UP, 1996. Print.

Lucas, Christopher J. *American Higher Education: A History*. New York: St. Martin's P, 1994. Print.

Mao, LuMing. *Reading Chinese Fortune Cookie: The Making of Chinese American Rhetoric*. Logan: Utah State UP, 2006. Print.

Mao, LuMing, and Morris Young, eds. *Representations: Doing Asian American Rhetoric*. Logan: Utah State UP, 2008. Print.

Margalit, Avishai. *The Ethics of Memory*. Cambridge: Harvard UP, 2002. Print.

Marinucci, Carla. "Little Saigon Opens Arms for McCain: Vietnamese Americans Dismiss His Use of Slur." *San Francisco Chronicle*, 2 March 2000, A3. LexisNexis Academic. Web. 10 Aug. 2006.

Marzluf, Phillip P. "'Diversity Stuff': Response to Margaret Himley and Christine Farris." *College Composition and Communication* 58.3 (2007): 465–69. Print.

Marzluf, Phillip P. "Diversity Writing: Natural Languages, Authentic Voices." *College Composition and Communication* 57.3 (2006): 503–22. Print.

Matsuda, Mari. "Looking to the Bottom: Critical Legal Studies and Reparations." *Critical Race Theory: The Key Writings That Informed the Movement*. 1987. Eds. Kimberlé Crenshaw, Neil Gotanda, Gary Peller, and Kendall Thomas. New York: The New Press, 1995. 63–79. Print.

Matsuda, Paul Kei. "The Myth of Linguistic Homogeneity in U.S. College Composition." *College English* 68.6 (2006): 637–51. Print.

Monaghan, E. Jennifer. *Learning to Read and Write in Colonial America*. Amherst: U of Massachusetts P, 2005. Print.

Moran, Rachel. "The Politics of Discretion: Federal Intervention in Bilingual Education." *California Law Review* 76.6 (1988): 1249–1352. JSTOR. Web. 25 May 2010.

Morimoto, Toyotomi. *Japanese Americans and Cultural Continuity: Maintaining Language and Heritage*. New York: Garland Publishing, 1997. Print.

Morrison, Toni. "Memory, Creation, and Writing." *Thought* 59.235 (1984): 385–90. Print.

Moss, Beverly J. *A Community Text Arises: A Literate Text and a Literacy Tradition in African-American Churches*. Cresskill, NJ: Hampton Press, 2003. Print.

Moss, Beverly J., ed. *Literacy across Communities*. Cresskill, NJ: Hampton Press, 1994. Print.

Murase, Mike. "Toward Barefoot Journalism." *Gidra* 6.4 (April 1974): 1, 34–46. Print.

Nakayama, Thomas K., and Robert L. Krizek. "Whiteness: A Strategic Rhetoric." *Quarterly Journal of Speech* 81 (1995): 291–309. Print.

National Commission on Asian American and Pacific Islander Research in Education. *Asian Americans and Pacific Islanders, Facts Not Fiction: Setting the Record Straight*. College Board, 2008. Web. 6 Oct. 2014.

Nevius, C. W., Marc Sandalow, and John Wildermuth. "McCain Criticized for Slur: He Says He'll Keep Using Term for Ex-Captors in Vietnam." *San Francisco Chronicle*, 18 Feb. 2000, A1. LexisNexis Academic. Web. 10 Aug. 2006.

Nguyen, Katherine. "Guide on Vietnamese Experience to Debut." *The Orange County Register*. 20 April 2002. Print.

Nishida, Mo. "Where Do We Go from Here?" *Gidra* 6.4 (April 1974): 20–21. Print.

Nora, Pierre. "Between Memory and History: *Les Lieux de Memoire*." *Representations* 26 (1989): 7–24. Print.

Omatsu, Glenn. "The 'Four Prisons' and the Movements of Liberation: Asian American Activism from the 1960s to the 1990s." *Contemporary Asian American: A Multidisciplinary Reader*. Eds. Min Zhou and James V. Gatewood. New York: New York UP, 2000. 80–114. Print.

Omi, Michael, and Howard Winant. *Racial Formation in the United States: From the 1960s to the 1990s*. 2nd ed. New York: Routledge, 1994. Print.

Palumbo-Liu, David. *Asian/American: Historical Crossings of a Racial Frontier*. Redwood City, CA: Stanford UP, 1999. Print.

Petersen, William. "Success Story, Japanese-American Style." *New York Times Magazine*, 9 Jan. 1966, sec. 6, pp. 20–43. ProQuest. Web. 1 May 2010.

Pham, Vu. "Antedating and Anchoring Vietnamese America: Toward a Vietnamese Historiography." *Amerasia Journal* 29.1 (2003): 137–52. Print.

Phan, Trần Hiếu. "Making, Teaching History." *Việt Tide* [Westminster] 3 Aug. 2001: 1. Print.

Powell, Malea. "Blood and Scholarship: One Mixed-Blood's Story." *Race, Rhetoric and Composition*. Ed. Keith Gilyard. Portsmouth, NH: Boynton/Cook-Heinemann, 1999. 1–16. Print.

Prendergast, Catherine. *Literacy and Racial Justice: The Politics of Learning after Brown v. Board of Education*. Carbondale: Southern Illinois UP, 2003. Print.

Prendergast, Catherine. "Race: The Absent Presence in Composition Studies." *College Composition and Communication* 50.1 (1998): 36–53. Print.

Ramirez, Anthony. "Word for Word/Asian Americans; McCain's Ethnic Slur: Gone, But Not Quite Forgotten." *New York Times*, 5 March 2000, sec. 4, p. 7, col. 1. LexisNexis Academic. Web. 10 Aug. 2006.

Rampton, Ben. *Crossing: Language and Ethnicity among Adolescents*. London: Longman, 1995. Print.

"Reagan Declares Colleges on Coast Face a Showdown." *New York Times*, 17 Dec. 1968, p. 39. ProQuest Historical Newspapers. Web. 12 Dec. 2007.

Reynolds, John Frederick. "Memory Issues in Composition Studies." *Rhetorical Memory and Delivery: Classical Concepts for Contemporary Composition and Communication*. Ed. John Frederick Reynolds. Hillsdale, NJ: Lawrence Erlbaum Associates, 1993. 1–16. Print.

Royster, Jacqueline Jones, and Jean C. Williams. "History in the Spaces Left: African American Presence and Narratives of Composition Studies." *College Composition and Communication* 50.4 (1999): 563–84. Print.

San Juan, E., Jr. "The Cult of Ethnicity and the Fetish of Pluralism: A Counterhegemonic Critique." *Cultural Critique* 18 (1991): 215–29. JSTOR. Web. 18 Dec. 2006.

Schmidt, Ronald. "Racialization and Language Policy: The Case of the U.S.A." *Multilingua* 21 (2002): 141–61. EBSCOhost Communication and Mass Media Complete. Web. 30 Nov. 2009.

Schroeder, Christopher L., Helen Fox, and Patricia Bizzell, eds. *ALT DIS: Alternative Discourses and the Academy*. Portsmouth, NH: Boynton/Cook–Heinemann, 2002. Print.

Scott, Joan W. "Multiculturalism and the Politics of Identity." *October* 61 (1992): 12–19. JSTOR. Web. 18 March 2007.

Scribner, Sylvia. "Literacy in Three Metaphors." *American Journal of Education* 93.1 (1984): 6–21. Print.

Shaughnessy, Mina P. *Errors and Expectations: A Guide for the Teacher of Basic Writing*. New York: Oxford UP, 1977.

Shuck, Gail. "Racializing the Nonnative English Speaker." *Journal of Language, Identity, and Education* 5.4 (2006): 259–76. Print.

Smitherman, Geneva. *Talkin and Testifyin: The Language of Black America*. Detroit: Wayne State UP, 1977. Print.

Steinman, Edward. "Historical Overview: Edward Steinman, Attorney Representing Kinney Kinmon Lau." Proceedings of the Symposium *Revisiting the Lau Decision: 20 Years After*. Ed. Sau-Lim Tsang. 3–4 Nov. 1994. 18–23. ARC Associates. Web. 15 Dec. 2008.

Stevens, Jr., Edward. *Literacy, Law, and Social Order*. DeKalb: Northern Illinois UP, 1988. Print.

Sugarman, Stephen D., and Ellen G. Widess. "Equal Protection for Non-English-Speaking School Children." *California Law Review* 62 (1974): 157–82. JSTOR. Web. 20 Dec. 2006.

Swiencicki, Jill. "The Rhetoric of Awareness Narratives." *College English* 68.4 (2006): 337–55. Print.

Szwed, John. "The Ethnography of Literacy." *Literacy: A Critical Sourcebook*. Eds. Ellen Cushman et al. Boston: Bedford/St. Martin's, 2001. 421–29. Print.

Tachiki, Amy, Eddie Wong, and Franklin Odo, eds. *Roots: An Asian American Reader*. Los Angeles: Regents of the U of California, 1971. Print.

Takagi, Dana. *The Retreat from Race: Asian Admissions and Racial Politics*. New Brunswick: Rutgers UP, 1992. Print.

Takaki, Ronald. *Strangers from a Different Shore: A History of Asian America*. Boston: Little Brown, 1989. Print.

Tamura, Eileen. "Asian Americans in the History of Education: An Historiographical Essay." *History of Education Quarterly* 41.1 (2001): 58–71. JSTOR. Web. 27 Jan. 2009.

Tamura, Eileen. "The English-Only Effort, the Anti-Japanese Campaign, and Language Acquisition in the Education of Japanese Americans in Hawaii, 1915–40." *History of Education Quarterly* 33.1 (1993): 37–58. JSTOR. Web. 27 Jan. 2009.

Tannen, Deborah. *Talking Voices: Repetition, Dialogue, and Imagery in Conversational Discourse*. Cambridge: Cambridge UP, 1989. Print.

Tatsukawa, Steve. "'Got Any Spare Change?' A Brief Glimpse at the Great Rise and Eventual Fall of the Modern American Underground Press." *Gidra* 5 (Feb. 1973): 11–13. Print.

Tran, Barbara, Monique T. D. Truong, and Luu Truong Khoi, eds. *Watermark: Vietnamese American Poetry and Prose*. New York: Asian American Writers' Workshop, 1998. Print.

Umemoto, Karen. "'On Strike!' San Francisco State College Strike, 1968–1969: The Role of Asian American Students." *Contemporary Asian American: A Multidisciplinary Reader*. Eds. Min Zhou and James V. Gatewood. New York: New York UP, 2000. 49–79. Print.

United States. Commission on Civil Rights. *A Better Chance to Learn: Bilingual-Bicultural Education*. Washington, DC: Clearinghouse Publication No. 51, 1975. Print.

United States. Office for Civil Rights, Dept. of Health, Education, and Welfare. J. Stanley Pottinger. "Identification of Discrimination and Denial of Services on the Basis of National Origin." Memorandum to School Districts with More Than Five Percent National Origin-Minority Group Children. 25 May 1970. Web. 12 Oct. 2007.

Uyematsu, Amy. "The Emergence of Yellow Power in America." *Gidra* 1.7 (Oct. 1969): 8–11. Print.

Vietnamese American Curriculum Project Committee. *Vietnamese Americans: Lessons in American History, An Interdisciplinary Curriculum and Resource Guide.* Garden Grove, CA: Orange County Asian and Pacific Islander Community Alliance, 2001. Print.

Villanueva, Victor. *Bootstraps: From an American Academic of Color.* Urbana, IL: National Council of Teachers of English, 1993. Print.

Võ, Linda Trinh. *Mobilizing an Asian American Community.* Philadelphia: Temple UP, 2004. Print.

Wang, L. Ling-Chi. "Historical Overview: Ling-chi Wang, Community Leader for the *Lau* Lawsuit." Proceedings of the Symposium *Revisiting the Lau Decision: 20 Years After.* Ed. Sau-Lim Tsang. 3–4 Nov. 1994. 3–6. ARC Associates. Web. 15 Dec. 2008.

Wang, L. Ling-Chi. "*Lau v. Nichols*: History of a Struggle for Equal and Quality Education." 1976. *The Asian American Educational Experience: A Sourcebook for Teachers and Students.* Eds. Don T. Nakanishi and Tina Yamano Nishida. New York: Routledge, 1995. 58–91. Print.

Wang, L. Ling-Chi. "*Lau v. Nichols*: The Right of Limited English-Speaking Students." *Amerasia* 2.2 (1974): 16–45. Print.

Wei, William. *The Asian American Movement.* Philadelphia: Temple UP, 1993. Print.

Welch, Kathleen. "Reconfiguring Writing and Delivery in Secondary Orality." *Rhetorical Memory and Delivery: Classical Concepts for Contemporary Composition and Communication.* Ed. John Frederick Reynolds. Hillsdale, NJ: Lawrence Erlbaum Associates, 1993. 17–30. Print.

Who Killed Vincent Chin? Dir. Christina Choy. Detroit: Film News Now Foundation & WTVS, 1988. DVD.

Williams, Patricia. *The Alchemy of Race and Rights.* Cambridge: Harvard UP, 1992. Print.

Winans, Amy E. "Local Pedagogies and Race: Interrogating White Safety in the Rural College Classroom." *College English* 67.3 (2005): 253–73. Print.

Winant, Howard. *The New Politics of Race: Globalism, Difference, Justice.* Minneapolis: U of Minnesota P, 2004. Print.

Wollenberg, Charles. *All Deliberate Speed: Segregation and Exclusion in California Schools, 1855–1975.* Berkeley: U of California P, 1976. Print.

Yamamoto, Eric K. *Interracial Justice: Conflict and Reconciliation in Post–Civil Rights America.* New York: New York UP, 1999. Print.

Yates, Francis. *The Art of Memory.* Chicago: U of Chicago P, 1966. Print.

Yeh-Lo, I. M. "UCLA Class on 'Orientals in America.'" *Gidra* 1.2 (May 1969): 6. Print.

Yoo, David K. "Testing Assumptions: IQ, Japanese Americans, and the Model Minority Myth in the 1920s and 1930s." *Remapping Asian American History.* Ed. Sucheng Chan. Walnut Creek, CA: Altamira P, 2003. 69–87. Print.

Young, James E. *The Texture of Memory: Holocaust Memorials and Meaning.* New Haven: Yale UP, 1993. Print.

Young, Morris. *Minor Re/Visions: Asian American Literacy Narratives as a Rhetoric of Citizenship.* Carbondale: Southern Illinois UP, 2004. Print.

Young, Morris. "Standard English and Student Bodies: Institutionalizing Race and Literacy in Hawai'i." *College English* 64.4 (2002): 405–31. Print.

Zenger, Amy A. "Race, Composition, and 'Our English': Performing the Mother Tongue in a Daily Theme Assignment at Harvard, 1886–87." *Rhetoric Review* 23.4 (2004): 332–49. Print.

Zhou, Min and Carl L. Bankston. *Growing up American: How Vietnamese Children Adapt to Life in the United States.* New York: Russell Sage Foundation, 1998. Print.

Index

AAVE. *See* African American Vernacular English (AAVE)

Adams, John, 6

African Americans, 7, 8, 12, 15, 27, 32, 58, 141; percent of student body, 86, 109; Petersen and, 37, 38. *See also Brown v. Board of Education* (1954)

African American Studies, 33

African American Vernacular English (AAVE), 62, 162

Agent Orange, 92

Alison (VAC member pseudonym), 88, 89, 93

Altbach, Philip, 71

Amerasia Journal, 67, 138

"American Gook" protest, 119–24, 129. *See also* Duc (VAC member pseudonym)

American Indians, 86. *See also* Native Americans

American Institute for Research, 52

Anaheim Union High School District, 138, 139, 142

Anglo-Saxon heritage, 33, 34

anti-Chinese immigration exclusion acts, 10, 12

Anzaldúa, Gloria, 33

Asian American Heritage Month, 143

Asian American Heritage Week, 82

Asian American movement, 15–18, 45, 69, 70

Asian American Political Alliance, 58, 74

Asian Americans, 11, 22, 29–35, 112, 113, 115, 141; and activism, 54–55, 58, 63, 159, 162; in the courts, 35–45; and education, 9–16, 38, 87; and language, 9, 19–20, 32, 33, 37; as students, 58, 73–74, 161. *See also Lau v. Nichols* (1974)

Asian American Studies Center, UCLA, 69

Asian Family Affair, The, 67

Asian Pacific Americans, 137, 138

Asian/Pacific Islanders, 86, 108

Attia (a Pakistani American junior), 75

Austin, J. L., 132, 133, 141

Australia, 10

Bankston, Carl L., 135–36

Baptist congregations, 8

Barnett, Timothy, 62

Baron, Dennis, 6

Bay Area, the, 67, 76

Bell, Derrick A., Jr., 46

Berkeley, 16, 62–63, 76

Bilingual Education Act, 44, 48, 51; (1968), 30, 44; (1974), 52; (1994), 52

Black culture, 129

Black English, 8, 32. *See also* African American Vernacular English (AAVE)

Blackmun, Justice Harold, 44

Black Panther Party, 67

Black Power movement, 29, 66

Blair, Hugh, 99

Bonilla-Silva, Eduardo, 100

Boy and Girl Scout Service's Learning for Life program, 161

Boyle Indian School, 7

Brand, Deborah, 4, 5

Bridge Magazine, 67

Brown v. Board of Education (1954), 27, 28, 29, 31, 35, 39, 40

Bryan (VAC member pseudonym), 87, 88, 91, 93, 98, 138, 139; and curriculum, 135, 137; and high school outreach, 98–103, 105–9

Bush, President George W., 142